BUSINESSMAN
FIRST

BUSINESSMAN FIRST

Remembering Henry G. Parks, Jr. 1916–1989
Capturing the Life of a Businessman Who Was African
American A Biography

Maurice W. Dorsey
2022

MAURICE W. DORSEY

Library of Congress Control Number:		2013918589
ISBN:	Hardcover	978-1-4931-1479-5
	Softcover	978-1-4931-1478-8
	Ebook	978-1-4931-1480-1

Rev. date: 10/22/2013

To order additional copies of this book, contact:
Xlibris LLC
1-888-795-4274
www.Xlibris.com
Orders@Xlibris.com
139730

To youth who someday want to go into business.

—Henry G. Parks Jr.

CONTENTS

Chapter 1   Businessman First 21

Apprenticeships and Early Career.. 21

Founding H. G. Parks Inc. 24

Financing H. G. Parks Inc.
and William Lloyd "Little Willie" Adams.............................. 25

USDA Inspection and Interstate Commerce.............................. 27

Advertising 28

Women at H. G. Parks Inc.. 31

Sales and Marketing 32

Publicity... 35

Training and Continued Learning.. 37

New Ventures... 40

Unionized Employees 42

New Products... 43

Phase II Expansion 43

Stock Issue... 45

Selling H. G. Parks Inc. to the Norin Corporation 46

Chapter 2   Corporate America... 49

First Pennsylvania Corporation 52

Magnavox Company... 53

Urban National Corporation / VNC Ventures............................ 53

W. R. Grace & Company Inc. 54

First Pennsylvania Bank NA... 55

Signal Companies... 55

Warner-Lambert Company 56

Chapter 3   Public Servant 58

    Elected to the Baltimore City Council, Fourth District 58

    Appointed President of the Board of Fire Commissioner for the
    City of Baltimore 61

Chapter 4   Giving Back 64

    National Urban League Inc. 64

    Alpha Phi Alpha Fraternity, Kappa Chapter 67

    National Association for the Advancement of Colored People
    (NAACP) 67

    Goucher College· 68

    Provident Hospital 68

    The Johns Hopkins University Center for Metropolitan Planning
    and Research 68

    Arena Players Inc. 69

    The National Dental Association 69

    The Interracial Council for Business Opportunity 69

    The United Negro College Fund 70

    Black Enterprise Magazine 70

Chapter 5   Honors and Recognitions 72

    The *New York Amsterdam News* 72

    Young Men's Christian Association (YMCA) 72

    The District of Columbia Chamber of Commerce 72

    The *New York Courier* 73

    The Small Business Men's League of Baltimore 73

    Philadelphia Citizens Selection Committee 73

    The Greater New Haven Business and Professional Men's
    Association 73

    The H. G. Parks Inc. Employees 74

    The Baltimore Frontiers Club 74

    Temple University 75

    Morgan State University 75

    Junior Achievement of Metropolitan Baltimore 76

    Arena Players Inc. 76

The Baltimore Marketing Association Inc. 76

The Greater Baltimore Committee 77

The United Negro College Fund Inc. 77

Warner-Lambert Company 78

Chapter 6   Family 79

Siblings 79

Marriage 80

Children and Grandchildren 82

Chapter 7   Finale 84

Honored Wounds 84

Healing Moments 86

Service of Memory 89

Epilogue 95

Appendix I 97

Appendix II 100

Appendix III 101

Appendix IV 103

Bibliography 107

List of Illustrations 111

PREFACE

The likelihood of Henry G. Parks and I meeting was orchestrated by the universe. With more than three decades' difference in our ages, and despite economic disparity, social class difference, and geographical separation, we became friends and had a relationship that survived for more than a decade.

The purpose of telling this story is to record a significant piece of African American history that may otherwise go unrecorded. It is also to keep a promise I made to him almost thirty years ago.

During the early 1900s, African Americans made significant accomplishments as inventors, scientists, abolitionists, entertainers, lawyers, and athletes. With the exception of Madame J. Walker, Barry Gordy, and John Johnson, few African Americans pioneered the American free-enterprise system to the extent of Henry G. Parks.

Henry and I met in Baltimore, Maryland, at a time when I was more or less starting a career, and he was more or less concluding his. I was completely captivated by his person and ambitious accomplishments. I was a Baltimore-unknown having started my life in rural Edgewood, Maryland. Henry and I spent hours together, usually over meals at his Baltimore home in the Bolton Hill neighborhood, Sess's—a local restaurant—or the Baltimore Center Club.

Although his home on Bolton Hill was far more exclusive than his previous home on Reservoir Street, it was simply appointed and housed numerous Haitian paintings he collected from his solo trips. There was a vinyl-covered sofa a friend had given him and a black leather directional director's chair I sold to him from the start of an interior design project that went south. I loved the sound of Henry's front doorbell, and I would often walk to the front courtyard entrance (that was a longer distance than from his rear entrance) just to hear the doorbell chime.

We talked incessantly about his life, both trials and tribulations, as he built the H. G. Parks Inc., and the happiness and struggles of his personal life. He introduced me to his family and closest personal friends. The contents of this book come from many of our conversations and his personal files that he passed on to me prior to his death.

This was a project that we worked on together. It was a project he wanted completed, and I was honored that he entrusted me, over several others, with the completion of this project. Henry provided me his lifetime's worth of personal files, including photographs of family, friends, and of his Baltimore City Council years; newspaper and magazine articles; advertising and marketing ads; copies of speeches; plaques and awards; personal letters from his daughter and grandson; and other memorabilia. I have kept this material for close to thirty years. Some items I photographed for my records and some have been donated to the Maryland Historical Society and to the Baltimore City Life Museums.

This book was written to celebrate Henry's life and his achievements, and to support aspiring business leaders, educators, community leaders, and neighborhood volunteers who consider going into business. With the exception of my personal interviews with family and friends, most of Henry's life is documented in a wide range of publications throughout the country. He was a highly successful businessman whom some called a marketing genius, a friend, a mentor, and a partial father figure to me. He inspired others and was universally admired. Hopefully, others can build on this biographical account and expand his story.

ACKNOWLEDGMENTS

I would like to acknowledge my life-defining people and individuals that have supported this project over the years:

Robert James Battjes, DSW
Archie Buffkins, PhD
Tamera Coleman
Curtiland Deville
Mr. and Mrs. James Roswell Dorsey Sr.
James Roswell Dorsey, Jr.
A. J. Dye, PhD
Raymond V. Haysbert Sr.
Daniel Huden, PhD
George Johnson, PhD
Grace G. Johnson
Mr. and Mrs. Luther Johnson
Marc Johnson
Robert Koopman, PhD
Daniel Kugler, PhD
Frederic Breed Mayo, PhD
Margaret D. Pagan
Cheryl Parks
Alice Pinderhughes
Pedro Ribalta
Robert E. Lee Ross
Evelyn Pasture Valentine, EdD
Mr. and Mrs. Clay Wilson
Silas Roscoe Young

INTRODUCTION

Considering the racial and economic discrimination against African Americans who wished to enter the American system of business, Henry G. Parks Jr. was before his time. He, with limited capital, navigated the American free-enterprise ideal, started a business, and within two decades, built a multimillion-dollar enterprise. Most people familiar with the slogan "More Parks' Sausages, Mom, Please!" did not know that he was Negro.

Born in Atlanta, Georgia, but raised in Dayton, Ohio, Henry was a man who loved his paternal grandmother, who lived with her son and daughter-in-law. She attended church regularly. She taught Henry to read the Bible, and by the time Henry was five years old, he was quoting the Bible. In his youth, many thought Henry would become a preacher. In his young adulthood, he still held this as a consideration, but it was a church sermon that persuaded him to change his mind and go into business instead.

His father worked as a bartender at the Biltmore Hotel in Ohio. During the depression of 1928, Henry's father asked his wife if she would join him in the workforce to help hold the family together, and she agreed. She became a maid in the same hotel that her husband worked. Henry was the oldest of the three children. He was twelve. Dayton, Ohio, was above the Mason-Dixon Line; African Americans were free, but getting a job was difficult, and it was referred to as the segregated north.

Henry was especially loved by his mother, Gainelle Esther Williams, born April 24, 1896. She was from Birmingham, Alabama. She enjoyed rose gardening and especially enjoyed the red, white, and pink as they bloomed in their season. Over the years, Henry learned to love them just as much. Henry learned to play tennis and to swim at the Young Men's Christian Association (YMCA). He was a lifeguard at the pool. He taught his mother both sports.

Henry was endeared to his mother, and tears would come to his eyes when he reflected on her memory as I interviewed him. He said she worked hard. She died of Parkinson's disease. This was a sad recollection for Henry. His sister Vera, in an interview, said, "Henry moved mother to Baltimore so she could go to the Johns Hopkins Hospital. She got the best of care."

Henry's relationship with his father, Henry Sr. (born August 14, 1890, in Atlanta, Georgia), was strained in his childhood and young adulthood. First,

Henry Sr. thought his son's activities with his mother were not masculine. Second, in regard to swimming and tennis, his father did not believe these were serious sports, and especially not for Negro men.

Henry Sr. liked to fish and hunt, but he never took Henry with him. However, when he returned from his solo hunting trips, Henry was charged with cleaning his father's catch of fish and wildlife. This was a punishment for being so close to his mother and not attaching to his father as was expected.

In addition to hunting and fishing, Henry Sr. owned hound dogs for sport, and Henry was charged with walking and cleaning up behind them. Henry disliked these chores and disliked his father for making him perform them. In these instances, Henry's mother could not protect her son.

On one occasion, while Henry was walking the dogs, one of the hunting dogs broke away and was lost. His father got very angry. Henry Sr. was very strong. He knew that his son loved his tennis equipment and worked hard and saved his money to purchase it. Henry Sr. located the tennis racket, took out his penknife, and cut out the center netting from the racket. He cut up Henry's tennis shoes too. Henry was a sensitive son. Tears streamed down his face, and under his breath, he called his father a son of a bitch. When I met Henry fifty years later, he still called his father a son of a bitch when he thought of this incident.

In some father-son relationships, fathers feel that if the son does not follow a clear masculine model, it somehow reflects on them. Henry rooted his feelings of hurt and resentment toward his father, but simultaneously, these situations also fueled and strengthened his determination to be successful and not endure any more of his father's abuse.

Throughout his young adult years, Henry maintained that his father was punitive and abusive to him.

In his senior years, he learned how difficult life was and forgave his father. He acknowledged his family was poor, and his father worked hard. His father worked long hours and was never home. Henry eventually learned through his life experiences that he could not judge his father because he too worked long hours and was never home when building the H. G. Parks Inc. He gave his father credit for holding the family together.

Henry was tall, handsome, possessed an athletic built, was well dressed and well behaved, and was a scholarly student. He was a voracious reader and participated in numerous school and civic activities. He graduated from Garfield Elementary School. The primary school was segregated, but Henry felt the teachers cared about the students. The whites went to a brick school with central heating. Henry's school was made out of wood and was heated by a potbellied stove. Henry was an Eagle Scout, and the troop traveled to Canada for camping and hiking. Henry was at Garfield for six years before being moved to an integrated school for the next six years.

Henry maintained good grades throughout his school years. He played football but not very well. He played tennis very well and was the first Negro on the squad and team captain. He was even better at swimming, but the school would not let Henry on the team. Roosevelt High School had a white swimming pool and a colored swimming pool. Henry was hurt and disappointed. The colored children could play football but not basketball. The school had separate class officers: a set of officers for white students and a set of officers for colored students. The graduation exercises were integrated, but the class prom and picnic were separate—no mixing allowed. Henry graduated from Roosevelt High School in Dayton, Ohio, in 1934 with honors. The newspapers acknowledged he was the most outstanding student.

In Henry's adult life, he was repeatedly invited back to high school reunions and other "Class of 1934" school functions, but he never attended. Charles H. Miller, class of 1934, wrote to Henry numerous times over the years, but Henry never responded.

After a certain time in a Negro's life, race visibly enters the picture, and although Roosevelt High was integrated long before many public schools in the United States, Henry said he never felt he was treated fairly.

Although Henry was an outstanding student, no one in the family imagined Henry would be going to college because there was no money for it. Henry had learned early on that he was alone in the world, and if he wanted anything in life, he had to earn it himself and go along the path keeping his mouth shut. He had earned a scholarship from the National Athletic Scholarship Society of Secondary Schools to play football—although he was better in swimming and tennis, he was not accepted for those teams.

He worked throughout his school years, and he was saving his money to go to college. Little did he know, the money he was sending home for his parents to save for college was being spent to support the family household. When it was time to go to college, there was no money. This he attributed to his father. Brokenhearted and hurt, he could not enter Ohio State University in September as he had planned. He kept a positive attitude, continued to work, and used the scholarships he had earned and matriculated a year later. No longer did he give the money to his parents to keep.

Closely akin to his high school years, Henry was fully engaged in college life and earned good grades. He made the freshman swimming team. Because of his fair complexion, the coach did not recognize him as colored, at first, and he was told that he was the first colored on the team.

In 1936, he pledged and was inducted in the Alpha Phi Alpha Fraternity, Kappa Chapter, located in Columbus, Ohio. Walter S. Scott Jr. was president and Charles H. Wesley was general president. Henry became a life member in 1952.

Jesse Owens was Henry's off-campus roommate in a ramshackle house where all the Negroes lived. They lived about five blocks from the campus. Negro students could not live or eat on the campus.

Jesse was born in Oakville, Alabama, on September 1, 1913. Jesse was a sharecroppers' child and a great-grandson of slaves. He had never met a white person who did not own his every breath. He was three years older than Henry.

Charles Riley, Jesse's physical education teacher, got Jesse three jobs at Ohio State to pay his tuition and to earn enough money to send home to his father, which introduces a condition of Jesse's father agreeing with Mr. Riley. Jesse was needed at home to work the farm. Jesse waited tables, ran the elevator, and worked in the library. He was still an athletic success.

Adolf Hitler had armed his country against Jesse and supported his best athlete Luz Long. Hitler even walked out of the stadium when Jesse competed. Jesse won four gold medals in track and field events at the 1936 Berlin Olympics. Adolf Hitler was astounded by the victories.

The name of Jesse Owens is hammered in bronze and embedded in stone at the marathon gate of the Berlin Stadium. Jesse and Luz Long became great friends. Henry did not think of Jesse as academically bright. With regard to all of his accomplishments and accolades Jesse received, Henry said he was not treated any different from any other Negro. Jesse had practiced for ten years and run 4,500 miles but was still regarded as a nigger.

Henry frequently told the story of his college-placement adviser who advised him to go to South America, change his name, learn Spanish, and come back to the United States to get a job doing anything he wanted. As a Negro student with outstanding grades, his adviser knew he would not be able to land a job in the United States because of racial prejudice and discrimination—and especially in the field of marketing. Henry did not think his adviser meant any harm, but he was determined not to run from his ethnicity.

Henry sent his dirty clothes home in a cardboard box for his mother to wash. She would wash, starch, and iron everything Henry sent. Henry's father did not like his wife doing his son's dirty laundry. He resented Henry being in college and never thought he would amount to more than the Negro he was.

Henry's mother would return the clothes in the same box Henry had sent them; turning the box inside out, she sent the clothes back to Henry. Sometimes, she would send Henry some money. Henry loved his mother, and his mother loved him. Lottie Jones, his godmother, also sent a few dollars to Henry.

In his early years, he had his eye on removing all the negatives that he thought would get in his way of advancement in a competitive business world. He had learned in his business studies that being named after your father indicated lineage and that you were from somewhere. Being a junior added credibility in the business world, thus he took his father's middle name and added Jr., using this on his résumés. Henry did not remember until he applied for his first passport in

1969 that his given name at birth was Henry Faris Parks. Henry also learned that your business address was important, thus he used Atlanta, Georgia (where he was born), on his résumés over Dayton, Ohio, although he lived in Atlanta for only four months of his life. Long before John Molloy's book *Dress for Success*, Henry had mastered the rules of corporate dress for an African American while in high school and college.

In 1939, Henry graduated from the Ohio State University College of Commerce, earning a bachelor of science degree in marketing. He was president of the Interracial Society, Interfraternal Council, and the Alpha Phi Alpha Fraternity. He graduated with honors.

On March 7, 1983, Ohio State Office of Minority Affairs listed Henry in a publication entitled *They Came and They Conquered*, a who's who of the university minority alumni. Henry was listed fully credentialed.

Chronology

Born Henry Faris Parks, Atlanta, Georgia, 1916
Attended Garfield Elementary School, Dayton, Ohio, 1923
Graduated Roosevelt High School, Dayton, Ohio, 1934
Member of the National Urban League, 1935
Member, Alpha Phi Alpha Fraternity, 1936
Married Virginia Byrd, 1938
Graduated from the Ohio State University, 1939
Director, Resident War Production Training Center, Wilberforce, Ohio, 1939
National sales representative, Pabst Brewing Company, 1940
Part-owner, W. B. Graham Associates, 1942
Part-owner, Crayton's Sausage Company, 1948
Started H. G. Parks Inc. trading as Parks Sausage Company, 1951
Received USDA approval, 1952
Life member, Alpha Phi Alpha, 1952
Divorced Virginia Byrd, 1953
Life member of the National Association for the Advancement of Colored
    People (NAACP), 1955
Expanded to 2460 Woodbrook Avenue, 1956
Unionized employees, 1958
Elected to Baltimore City Council, 1963
Opened Parks Motor Rental, 1963
Sales peaked six million dollars, 1964
Joined Tuesday Publications, 1965
Opened plant at Camden Yard, 1967
Featured on the cover of *BusinessWeek*, 1968

Issued public stock, 1969

Time Southeast Asia News Tour, 1969

Elected to the board of trustees, Goucher College, 1969

Elected to the board of trustees, Provident Hospital, 1970

Elected to the board of directors, First Pennsylvania Corporation, 1971

Elected to the board of directors of Magnavox, 1971

Elected to the board of directors, VNC Ventures, 1971

Elected to the board of directors, W. R. Grace & Company, 1974

Time Middle East News Tour, 1975

Elected to the board of directors, First Pennsylvania Bank NA, 1975

Received honorary doctorate of law, Temple University, 1975

By 1975 H. G. Parks, Inc. never recorded a losing year since the day opened
    in 1951

Elected to the board of directors, Signal Companies, 1976

Parks Sausage sales reached $14 million, 1976

Received honorary doctorate of human letters, Morgan State University, 1976

Elected to the board of directors, Warner-Lambert, 1977

William Donald Schaefer, mayor of Baltimore, designated a Henry Parks Day
    in Baltimore, 1977

Sold Parks Sausage Company, 1977

Elected to the board of directors, First Pennsylvania Financial Services, 1978

Appointed president of the Baltimore Board of Fire Commissioners, 1981

Elected to the board of directors of Baltimore Arena Players, 1981

Designated Distinguished American by United States Congress, 1982

Received the Greater Baltimore Committee Jefferson Miller Award, 1983

Resigned as chairman of the board of H. G. Parks Inc., 1987

CHAPTER 1

Businessman First

She was my sponsor in a sense.
—Henry G. Parks Jr. referring to Dr. Mary McLeod Bethune

Apprenticeships and Early Career

After Henry graduated from Ohio State University with honors from the College of Commerce and a major in marketing, and as the only black in his class, there were jobs for all the white students, but no jobs for Henry in the field of business. Henry's adviser could not understand why Henry chose marketing as a field of study, knowing no one would hire him. Henry's placement adviser recommended that Henry go to South America, learn Spanish, change his name, and come back to the United States pretending to be of Spanish descent, and he could get a job anywhere he wanted. Henry didn't feel the guy meant any harm, but he was not running from his race.

Henry was employed by the National Youth Administration in Wilberforce, Ohio, as the director of the Resident War Production Training Center. Dr. Mary McLeod Bethune hired Henry and served as his mentor. She was forty-one years his senior and also a friend of Eleanor Roosevelt.

In this first job, he had fifty employees under him, and several hundred youth came through the program—youth that came from ghetto situations and trained in a residential facility for jobs in industry. The program was successful, and Henry was able to place many of the trainees in machine and auto mechanic shops. Henry was not only inspired by Dr. Bethune—"She was my sponsor in a sense." She gave Henry his first chance to try his hand at business management in a federal government setting. He worked in this position from 1939 to 1940.

Dr. Bethune used her friendship with Mrs. Roosevelt to get resources for the program. Mrs. Roosevelt was sympathetic to the plight of women and Negroes. When the Daughters of the American Revolution (DAR) barred Marian Anderson from singing in their Constitution Hall in Washington, DC, Eleanor Roosevelt publicly resigned from the DAR. Mrs. Roosevelt's resignation was a symbol for equality for women and Negroes. However, neither Eleanor nor President Roosevelt publicly spoke out against Jim Crow.

Significantly, in Henry's early years, he joined Pabst Brewing Company as a national sales representative. He developed a proposal to market the black community. Pabst hired Henry, but they scrapped his proposal. They thought the proposed plan for blacks that Henry was presenting would change their image. Race was not a line they were willing to cross to conduct business with the Negroes. However, they hired him because they wanted the black market and thought of methods other than what Henry had proposed.

Henry accepted the challenge, made friends, and persuaded pre-Amtrak dining car waiters and Pullman porters to add Pabst to the bar. They then, in turn, asked the crew chefs to order and stock Pabst. Budweiser was the only beer being stocked. In a short period, Henry became one of Pabst's top sales representatives. Pabst moved to becoming the top seller on the trains due to Henry's marketing strategy.

Henry employed a similar strategy on the West Coast in Los Angeles and Hollywood. In California, he worked the chauffeurs, butlers, houseboys, and others who did the food-and-beverage shopping for many of the celebrities.

With this coast-to-coast success, Henry should have been promoted to manager, but Pabst would not promote him because it would have caused conflict with the other white managers. Henry resigned from the company when they refused him a managerial position. After he left the company, they offered to double his salary but still would not negotiate a managerial position. I said, "Henry, that took nerve." He said to me with certainty, "Maurice, man? I can sell anything." Henry worked for Pabst from 1940 to 1942.

In 1941, the United States entered WWII after the Japanese bombed Pearl Harbor. At home, there were still issues for Negroes in areas of housing, health, employment, interstate transportation, and public accommodations. There were approximately 3,842 lynch recorded between 1889 and 1941.

In 1945, John H. Johnson published the first issue of *Ebony* magazine. In 1949, WERD was the first black-owned radio station that opened in Atlanta, Georgia; Wesley A. Brown became the first black graduate from the Annapolis Naval Academy. By 1950, Dr. Ralph J. Bunche was the first black awarded the Nobel Peace Prize, and Gwendolyn Brooks won the Pulitzer Prize for Poetry. Henry, still young and inspired, was feeling the energy of blacks making it big, and he maintained those desires from his childhood.

In 1946, President Truman created a President's Committee on Civil Rights. The 1947 report called for a broad range of policies against racism: eliminating discrimination and segregation in employment, housing, health facilities, interstate transportation, and public accommodations, implementing a law to make lynching a crime, the abolition of the poll tax, federal protection of voting rights, and executive orders against discrimination in the federal civil service and the armed forces.

From 1942 to 1950, Henry was part-owner of W. B. Graham Associates Inc. in New York City, a personal management company of two members. W. B. Graham had also worked for Pabst Brewing Company. Mr. Graham was older than Henry. Henry laughed and said, "I did all the work, and he kept all the money." Together, they performed theater bookings and provided public relations services.

This was the era when Jackie Robinson became the first black to play major league baseball. One of W. B. Graham's clients was Joe Louis. They did the promotion of a soft drink called the Joe Louis Punch. This was planned to be an alternative drink to Coca-Cola. Henry remarked it tasted awful, lost its color in the sun, and had no fizz. The product was not successful.

Marva Louis, wife of Joe Louis, was also a client of W. B. Graham Associates. She was a singer for a short period. Henry said she was good but not a great singer. Henry toured with her in thirty cities in forty days. This was one of the successful ventures of the consulting firm, but she, of course, got most of the money, and they received very little.

It was through Joe Louis that Henry met William Lloyd "Little Willie" Adams, a numbers runner in Baltimore and an entrepreneur and venture capitalist, who agreed to help finance H. G. Parks Inc. It was Mr. Adams who suggested Henry move from New York to Baltimore and work in the real estate field, and Henry accepted. Eventually, Mr. Adams agreed to finance H. G. Parks Inc., trading as Parks Sausage Company, during Henry's second year of operation.

In 1948, while holding part-ownership in W. B. Graham, Henry resigned and moved back to Ohio to work at Crayton's Southern Sausage Company of Cleveland, Ohio. Henry and Mr. Adams bought into the company. Leroy Crayton was president and had controlling ownership. Henry liked the company and had important responsibilities. The company grew, and Henry had a plan to expand the sausage company, similar to his youthful ideas about Pabst. Mr. Crayton did not want to expand and stopped Henry.

Henry left Crayton's Southern Sausage Company with plans to open his own business. It was Mr. Adams who suggested Henry come to Baltimore. Upon arrival, Henry worked with Mr. Adams in real estate and became a licensed real estate broker with Mr. Adams, who was already doing this type of work. Henry sold a few homes to Negroes on Fulton Avenue in Baltimore, a street that had been of all white residents. Henry later became part-owner of two drugstores with packaged goods and a pharmacy in the black community of Turner Station. At the same time, he went into business owning a cinderblock manufacturing company. He laughed and said, "I just about went bankrupt!" He was doing all these jobs at once and maintaining an office in New York as well. Henry then decided that he needed to settle down and do one thing.

Before founding H. G. Parks Inc., Henry approached Mr. Albert Goetze, the owner of a local meat-packing company in Baltimore, to offer an idea on developing a low-priced line of pork products to sell to the Negro community in the inner city. Henry said, "Old Mr. Goetze gave me my best advice. He told me to go out and form my own company. And so I did!" At that time, Henry did not even dream that he would be as successful as he turned out to be.

Founding H. G. Parks Inc.

To succeed in business, do something better.
—Henry G. Parks Jr.

H. G. Parks Inc. was founded in 1951 at the rear of 2509 Pennsylvania Avenue, Baltimore, Maryland, with two employees. This location was in an alley and in a place that was very much considered a ghetto. Occupying the front of the building was the Reliable Liquor Company. A guy named Smitty owned the building and told Henry to write up his own building lease and to pay what he thought the rent should be. "I will sign it whatever you write!" Henry said he did not know how to write a lease, but he did a pretty good job. He tiled the walls, purchased a boiler and other used equipment, and started business. Henry said he had the notion of manufacturing Southern foods because they have a distinctive taste and because they are made with less expensive cuts of meat. Henry was thirty-five years old.

H. G. Parks Inc. started servicing the Baltimore Negro community. Sausages were made early in the morning and sold by canvassing local grocery stores in the afternoon. The company got repeat calls for the product, and sales grew. Henry said he nearly lost it all in the first couple of years because he could not get financing whereby he could produce on a larger scale to meet the increasing demand. He applied repeatedly for bank loans and was rejected with no explanation. He was not deterred.

His friends thought he had a lot of nerve to undertake a business like pork manufacturing. There were many well-established meat-packing companies marketing sausage in the United States and in the region. As a victim of racial segregation and oppression, Henry's attitude was that "black America had nothing to run from but a lot to run toward." And run toward is what he did. His attitude and positive outlook were his saving grace. He learned through his relationship with his father and his experience at Roosevelt High School in Dayton, Ohio, that negativity did not serve anyone well.

During Henry's start-up years, Rosa Parks, in December 1955, refused to relinquish her seat on a city bus in Montgomery, Alabama. This incident inspired the bus boycott in Montgomery, Alabama that was led by Martin Luther King.

Many blacks in the country did not have the positive attitude toward life that Henry did in the segregated north.

As sales increased for H. G. Parks Inc., Henry was enabled to expand and move from his Pennsylvania Avenue location to 2460 Woodbrook Avenue. At this location, he could better meet the demand of his expanding clientele. The building, formerly a dairy plant, was equipped with reconditioned machinery and furniture but met his space needs.

Very early in the development of the company, he established the aims of H. G. Parks Inc. The aim for the president and all the employees was to make Parks Sausage a source of mutual pride in the communities where they were located. As the company grew, it would mean more pay checks, more customers, more economic security for people, and would serve as an inspiration to youth who wished to someday go into business. Parks employees were respected members of their neighborhoods. They participated in community action events of the National Association for the Advancement of Colored People (NAACP), the March of Dimes, and the fight against juvenile delinquency.

Financing H. G. Parks Inc.
and William Lloyd "Little Willie" Adams

I paid Willie every cent that I owed to him.
—Henry G. Parks Jr.

Through Henry's association with Joe Louis, who held the world heavyweight title in 1937, he met William Lloyd "Little Willie" Adams. The three were a trio. Joe Louis would visit Henry at the plant just to see what was going on. Sidney Poitier also visited the plant, photographed in *JET* magazine—it is an image of Negro men supporting Negro men.

Mr. Adams, a Negro and uneducated, was, by age sixteen, a low-level numbers runner for an illegal lottery operation on the streets of Baltimore. He was shrewd when it came to handling and saving money.

Mr. Adams was the son of a sharecropper from Zebulon, North Carolina. He developed a wide network of business and political contacts across Baltimore. His business interests were in real estate, liquor stores, mortuaries, apartment buildings, and beauty parlors. When African Americans could not go to banks, Mr. Adams helped them financially to get the money they needed to start a business. The condition was that Mr. Adams would have a 51 percent stake in the business, no matter how small his personal investment. That did not sound like a deal to me!

Procuring financing for a small business, however, was tough for most African Americans. Mr. Adams was the owner of Little Willie's Inn located at Druid Hill

Avenue and Whitelock Street in 1935. The inn was bombed in 1938 by alleged Philadelphia gangsters. The gangsters wanted 5 percent of the cut from Mr. Adams's numbers business. When Mr. Adams refused to pay, they bombed his inn.

During that time, Mr. Adams's wealth was derived principally from illegal lotteries that he operated. The Pimlico Race Course results determined the winning three numbers. His reputation throughout the city was that he always paid out what he owed. He was hailed and honored by many.

Mr. Adams owned Adams Realty Brokers, located on Pennsylvania Avenue in 1939, and the Club Casino in 1940. Henry and Mr. Adams bought in to the Crayton's Southern Sausage Company of Cleveland, Ohio. When there was a disagreement over the expansion of the business (Mr. Leroy Crayton, who owned majority interest in his company, refused to expand), it was then that Henry and Mr. Adams sold their interest in Crayton's Sausage and moved to Baltimore.

Recognizing Henry's determined interest in business, Mr. Adams suggested Henry move to Baltimore to manage Mr. Adams's interest. For a brief period, he worked with Mr. Adams but subsequently used his share of the proceeds from the Crayton's Sausage Company along with monies from savings, mortgaging his house, and a life insurance policy to start H. G. Parks Inc.

In Henry's second year of operation, Mr. Adams provided the necessary capital for Henry to expand H. G. Parks Inc. Mr. Adams then became a silent partner in the enterprise and remained so until the company was sold.

Henry needed Mr. Adams's money to accomplish what he wanted to accomplish, but hated the stigma associated with Mr. Adams being a numbers runner. Mr. Adams was a successful businessman but memories of his illegal activities lingered. Henry wanted to own and operate a legitimate business and to clearly have his business separated from the monies he borrowed and fully paid to Mr. Adams. In an interview, I brought up the issue of Mr. Adams's notorious illegal operations of the past. Henry hotly said, "I paid Willie every cent that I owed to him." I interpreted this as "I run a legitimate business."

Henry and Mr. Adams were loyal, lifelong business partners. Henry benefited over the years from Mr. Adams's successful business ventures, such as the A&R Development Corporation, a national real estate company. Mr. Adams was also the founder of the HUB Organization Inc. The goal of the HUB was to obtain economic parity in the African American business community by becoming distributors, wholesalers, and procurement contractors.

Henry openly admitted he got his hands dirty sometimes. He said, "And if I offended some people, they damned well needed to be offended," and "I have no apology to make to anybody." Mr. Adams's share in H. G. Parks Inc. was reduced over the years, but he continued to sit on the Parks board of directors and owned 26 percent of the stock.

Henry was very fond of Mr. Adams's wife, Victorine. She was an educator and the first black woman to serve on the Baltimore City Council. She founded

Women Power, a group designed to get colored women involved in politics and civic work. Mrs. Adams was the founder of the Colored Women's Democratic Campaign Committee of Maryland and was well-known for her work with the Fuel Fund, a state government program designed to assist residents in paying their energy bills.

In addition to making a name of her own, Henry admired the role Mrs. Adams played as wife during her husband's drawn-out legal difficulties. Mr. Adams had some threatening issues with the law. Henry deeply admired how Mrs. Adams stood by her husband during these times. Henry said, "A wife should stand by her husband," and that "Business is risky."

Mr. Adams was saluted by the Associated Black Charities and other groups around the city for his contribution to local African American business leaders. Former mayor Kurt L. Schmoke stated, "For many years he was the most 'reliable bank' that African Americans could go to in order to start and continue to operate a business." Former mayor Thomas J. D'Alesandro III stated, "Little Willie was an institution in Baltimore. And as far as the black community was concerned, he brought black entrepreneurs into the formerly all-white business community . . . He was also a political power in his own right and had a tremendous network."

Henry never attempted to get federal financing for H. G. Parks Inc. Many banks had turned him down, but when he planned the second expansion for business, the Maryland National Bank financed the construction of his new plant in Camden Yards, the current site of Baltimore Stadium.

Although Henry served on the board of directors for the First Pennsylvania Bank, the banks of Baltimore never invited Henry to serve on their boards. He was described as being "Little Willie's" man. Baltimore bankers accepted Henry but not his association with Mr. Adams.

USDA Inspection and Interstate Commerce

A business owned and controlled by Negroes.
—the *Pittsburgh Courier*

Sales were low, and he needed to expand his market. With his Ohio State University education and his experience with Crayton's Southern Sausage Company, he wanted to bring safety and quality to his pork products as well as market across state lines. In 1952, he requested a USDA meat inspection of his plant. Within a reasonable time, he received the United States Department of Agriculture (USDA) seal of approval. This inspection took place at the plant located in the alley on Pennsylvania Avenue in Baltimore. Having the USDA seal of approval indicated quality to consumers.

Carl Murphy, president of the *Afro-American* newspaper congratulated Henry on the federal inspection of his plant. The *Pittsburgh Courier* described it as "A business owned and controlled by Negroes." This was a proud moment in the Negro community.

Henry made plans to expand his market as he attempted at Pabst and Crayton's Southern Sausage. He expanded to south Washington, DC, first then moved slowly northward on the Eastern Seaboard. Although sales were low in Baltimore, Baltimore was to remain the headquarters.

Distribution centers were established in Philadelphia; Pennsylvania, which also served Delaware; New York, which served New Jersey; and West Haven, Connecticut, serving the Boston, Massachusetts, area. He had a distribution center built in a southern state, but just as it was fully stocked, it was burned to the ground. After the incident, he had a vision for growth and expansion in Chicago, Illinois, and Detroit, Michigan, and was marketing through the *Tuesday Magazine* supplement connections, but after the publication failed, he moved to other ventures.

Advertising

More Parks' Sausages, Mom, Please!
—Leon Shaffer Golnick

H. G. Parks Inc. advertised and marketed Parks's famous flavor and USDA seal of approval to the general public, thus integrating market sales. The USDA seal implied quality to consumers, and Henry taste-tested the sausage each day to ensure consistency. He said he noticed if the taste varied even slightly.

Henry advertised in every venue from homemade to full-blown professional advertising. Few Negro firms saw a need to establish a trade character. However, Henry saw that establishing a trade character gave identity and more familiarity with the product.

Early in the company's advertising, "Parky," a real-life trade personality was introduced. Parky represented the company at trade shows, special events, and community and children's affairs. Parky would walk the streets giving out Parks Sausage of the mild variety. Parky became the trademark of Parks Sausage early on in the company's advertising. Later, "Sparky" was added for the spicy and extra spicy products, followed by the "Sparketts" and "Wonder Mouse," all approaches for getting the name to the public. Henry wanted to appeal to adults and children.

Parks Sausage was being advertised throughout the Baltimore-Washington metropolitan area at home shows, strategically placing printed fact sheets about the product with recipes and by hosting and sponsoring metropolitan-wide food-tasting events. Henry had young ladies, both white and Negro, conducting taste tests in grocery stores, and regularly displayed wallet-sized copies of the Parks Creed for consumers to take home—adding to increased trust and visibility.

The Parks Creed stated:

> *I know that I am a valuable member of a strong, solid team that is constantly building a better company.*
>
> *I know that the Parks Company is trusted and respected because each one of us is trusted and respected.*
>
> *I know that the slightest mistake or misjudgment made by any one of us will hurt all of us.*
>
> *I know that the very life of the Parks Company depends on how I, myself, look and speak and perform my duties.*
>
> *I know that the company is good, bad or indifferent is exactly as I am good, bad, or indifferent.*
>
> *I know that I must always remember and uphold qualities which have made me and my company successful: personal integrity, appearance, responsibility, kindness, and service.*
>
> *Finally, I know that everyone I meet, I am the Parks Company.*

During the period when sales were suffering in Baltimore, Henry decided to expand and move beyond the Baltimore area. Henry decided to market regionally, and his first location was Washington, DC. In 1953, Henry sent a carton of pork sausage to the White House. President and First Lady Eisenhower were residents. Although President Eisenhower was not the best political friend to Negroes collectively, he and the First Lady sent a thank-you letter and a positive and affirming reply to Henry. Henry used the reply letter from the President and First Lady of the United States as an advertisement to market Parks Sausage to the District of Columbia and the surrounding Maryland and Virginia supermarkets.

Some chain stores wanted to restrict his product to the black community, but Henry wanted every customer—urban, suburban, black, Jewish, and Italian markets. Henry believed everybody could enjoy the good taste of a piece of sausage from time to time. After DC, he moved northward to Philadelphia and up the East Coast. Sales in Baltimore were always lower than other locations. Baltimoreans did not like to pay premium prices for products.

On January 15, 1955, Parks Sausage and the Washington newspaper *Spotlight* sponsored its first Chitterlings King or Queen Eating Contest and Feast at the Roosevelt Hotel, 2101 Sixteenth Street NW, Washington, DC. The event was advertised throughout the city, but the Kingman Park Civic Association took action at the Spingarn Senior High School in condemning the event, thinking Negroes should elevate themselves from such demeaning events.

Henry personally and quickly met with members of the group to perform damage control from the negative press. He informed the members of the association of the freshness of his pure pork products, the nutritional value, the quality of his products, the grade of meat used in his products; he described how the products were prepared, the products' guarantee, how the product did not taste greasy, he described how the product held together when frozen, the cleanliness of the plant, the staff who handled the products, and the products' USDA seal of approval. The chitterlings contest was not designed to be demeaning but instead a means to attract attention to the product. Henry's presentation was received well by the Kingman Park association, but he didn't have future contests, agreeing with some of the association members' perceptions.

H. G. Parks Inc. was the first African American firm to advertise in a World Series. Parks Sausage advertisements appeared at one of the seven games between the Brooklyn Dodgers and the New York Yankees in 1955.

By 1957, Parks Sausages advertisements appeared in the *Washington Post*, the *Philadelphia Inquirer*, the *Philadelphia Daily News*, and the *Philadelphia Tribune*. Television advertisements for Wonder Mouse appeared by October of the same year. Radio fact sheets for WDRC, Hartford, Connecticut were aired. The H. G. Parks Inc. participated in the Philadelphia Home Show on April 29, 1958.

A new advertisement campaign "Operation Impact" began in 1958. It was a hard-hitting, hard-selling, saturating radio campaign in major marketing areas. Millions of people along the East Coast and the Tri-County area and Detroit metropolitan area would hear these advertisements. There were point-of-purchase displays, in-store promotions, demonstrations, and local newspaper advertising. Parks employees were highlighted in some of these promotions.

In 1962, the Parks Sausage Company received the award of superiority for radio commercials by Blair Radio National Survey. In 1963, *Sponsor*, the weekly magazine that radio and television advertisers use, rated the Parks Sausage in the top ten radio commercials named in a pulse study for Blair Radio. H. G. Parks Inc. was among other winners such as Chevrolet, Coca-Cola, Dodge, Kellogg's Corn Flakes, Pepsi Cola, V8 Juice, Ford Motors, and Pall Mall cigarettes.

It was not until 1965 (through much of the hard work and brilliant advertising of Leon Shaffer Golnick, president of the agency bearing his name) that Henry's company grew to a multimillion-dollar manufacturing industry. Mr. Golnick's firm created the advertisement "More Parks' Sausages, Mom." The "Please!" was added later.

Originally, the commercial did not use a professional artist. It was simply a radio advertisement where Lee Case, WCBM announcer, and his son Josh teamed up on a commercial that made the "ten best" list of the Radio Advertising Bureau. Josh Case, aged five, became a member of the American Federation of Television and Radio Artists; the youngest one in the Baltimore-Washington chapter. This advertising integrated H. G. Parks's market. Parks Sausage no longer marketed only the Negro community but the general community. Most consumers never knew H. G. Parks Inc. was a Negro-owned company. Henry wanted to keep it that way. He wanted only to sell a good product to the consumer for a good price and on the same terms as any other businessman in America.

Leading publications such as *Life* magazine, *Look* magazine, *McCall's Magazine*, and *Reader's Digest* carried Parks Sausage advertisements. By September, Foster and Kleiser covered East Coast cities with billboards and heavily throughout New York's Manhattan, Queens, Bronx, and Brooklyn.

The Radio Advertising Bureau (RAB) Inc. that reported the trends, case histories, and successful ideas of radio advertisers and agencies in America's major markets wrote, "Parks Sausages, for 13 years, has put 85% to 100% of its advertising budget into radio, has made the phrase 'More Parks' Sausages, Mom' household words in its distribution area. Currently 90% of Parks budget is in radio in Philadelphia, Pennsylvania, New York, Hartford, Connecticut, Springfield, Massachusetts, and New Jersey."

Mr. Golnick, president of the advertising agency, told RAB, "As a direct result of our new commercials for Parks, sales have increased 35% in New Jersey, 26% in New York, and 16% in Philadelphia."

Women at H. G. Parks Inc.

Get accustomed to seeing black faces in high places.
—Dr. Mary McLeod Bethune

Holding much respect for his grandmother, mother, and women leaders like Dr. Mary McLeod Bethune, Henry did not discriminate toward women.

Betty Friedan was the first president of the National Organization for Women (NOW) in 1966. Henry was ahead of most CEOs on the issues of equality for women in the workplace.

From the first day of business in 1951, Henry included women in the production, sales, and administrative development of H. G. Parks Inc. Women talked to the dealers and consumers about the product. Saleswomen would go into Negro beauty parlors and grocery stores as salesmen would go into barbershops and shoe-shine stands to market the product.

He supported women leaders such as Victorine Adams, wife of William Lloyd "Little Willie" Adams, who served on the Baltimore City Council and was founder of an organization called Women Power. Mrs. Adams stated that Henry was a frequent contributor to Women Power Inc., a group she set up in 1958 to get black women into politics and registered to vote.

It was not until March 22, 1972, that Congress passed the Equal Rights Amendment to guarantee sex equality. By 1973, thirty of the necessary thirty-eight states endorsed the amendment, but it ultimately failed to win ratification. In 1975, the Supreme Court decided *Frontiero v. Richardson,* and four justices held that classifications based on sex should be treated with the same degree of suspicion as those based on race.

Henry supported woman publisher Mrs. Robert L. Vann, president and publisher of the *Courier of Philadelphia.*

In 1958, H. G. Parks Inc. hosted a Ladies' Day Brunch at the Gotham Hotel, Ebony Room 111, Orchestra Place in Michigan. Henry was principal speaker and spoke of how he was encouraged by the late Dr. Mary McLeod Bethune, who employed and mentored him in his early career. "She gave much of the inspiration to move forward and to make an independent venture into business. Dr. Bethune continued to impress upon me things can get done with determination."

Henry was appointed to the board of trustees of Goucher College, an all-women liberal arts college, in 1959.

Women Power presented Henry an award in 1975 for his outstanding community efforts to advance and support women issues.

In a 1977 Sunday *New York Times* article, Henry stated, "We have gone beyond the time of protest marches against discrimination . . . I want to see that young people blacks, and other minorities of whatever race, including women are not frustrated in their expectations of acceptance and advancement."

Sales and Marketing

I am not interested in nigger sausage.

—A retailer

One of Henry's mottoes was "If you are going to remain in business, you must make reasonable profit. It could not be a show profession."

H. G. Parks Inc. driver-salesmen drove brightly colored red-white-blue-and-yellow Parks Sausage trucks throughout metropolitan areas of the East Coast. As the red-white-blue-and-yellow became more familiar, so did the product. Employees who worked for Henry trusted where he was leading them and were assured they had a future with the company.

Sales employees were encouraged to market the American free-enterprise ideal and to represent the growing participation of blacks in the American economy. Henry stated, "It is the obligation of any company doing business with the public to allow them to know as much about the company as possible. It is our desire not only to be good neighbors in the communities but, equally important, to keep the public informed as to who we are and what our plans for the future entail." Employees were encouraged to carry a wallet card of the Parks Creed to keep them familiar with the aims of the company.

In addition to their professional labors, employees were encouraged to make contributions to the communities where they lived. The company created a speakers bureau whereby employees could go to churches, civic associations, social, and fraternal organizations to spread goodwill and fully engage in the betterment of neighborhoods.

Parks Sausage Company would follow up with community leaders and host taste-testing and breakfast events at a time when Parks executives would share the importance of economic development and the manufacturing industry's relationship to the Negro community.

By 1955, *Sepia* magazine reported that H. G. Parks Inc. employed more than sixty employees serving Maryland, the District of Columbia, Virginia, New Jersey, Delaware, Pennsylvania, and New York.

Congress passed the Civil Rights Act of 1964, and President Johnson signed it. The act outlaws race and gender discrimination in voting, public accommodations, and employment. Title VI prohibits discrimination in education and becomes a tool for desegregation. Sales at H. G. Parks Inc. peaked six million by 1964.

By 1968, 75 percent of the H. G. Parks Inc. market was white. New York sold more of his products than Baltimore. Henry and I would laugh when he told the story of a meat buyer who said to Henry as Henry was trying to make a sale, "I am not interested in nigger sausage." Henry replied, "I am not trying to sell you one. So now let's talk business." Henry made the sale.

Safeway stores in Washington, DC, notified Henry on September 5, 1968, that he was authorized to stock Parks Sausage in their stores. Safeway was the first chain of food stores to carry Parks Sausage. With Safeway's endorsements, the Parks Sausage market became broader. This was a huge success. With this endorsement, Parks Sausage gained exposure in the *New York Times*, the *Wall Street Journal*, and *BusinessWeek*. He had captured the attention of corporate America.

Lyndon B. Johnson won the presidential election in November 1968. Blacks overwhelmingly supported Johnson, which signaled the beginning of a fundamental realignment in American politics. Blacks shifted their allegiance to the Democratic Party over the next thirty years while the white south became increasingly more Republican. Martin Luther King was awarded the Nobel Peace Prize the following month.

By 1975, H. G. Parks Inc. built from nothing to a $12-million-a-year business. According to an article in *Black Enterprise* magazine, in the third annual list of the top one hundred largest black-owned businesses in the United States, H. G. Parks Inc. was rated the seventh. Motown Industries (Los Angeles, California), Johnson Publishing Company Inc. (Chicago, Illinois), and Johnson Products Co. Inc. (Chicago, Illinois) were one, two, and three, respectively. Henry was a mentor to Earl Graves, publisher of *Black Enterprise* magazine.

When Safeway announced plans to revert to warehouse sales rather than direct sales, Henry found the news quite disturbing. On July 29, 1976, he wrote to R. V. Haysbert Sr., the president, an internal memo on the strength of the long-term relationship with Safeway and how this change would be disruptive to business. H. G. Parks Inc. was now selling to Domino's Pizza and Pizza Hut, which was a large chunk of the company's market. Henry's concerns were the issues of managing freshness control, cost, waste and spoilage control, lost sales, bar coded and dated merchandise, flexibility to fit each store's profile, and maximum effectiveness on promotions.

As of August 1976, the distribution pattern of the sausage industry was Bob Evans, Green Hill, and Parks as the only three direct-fresh producers, compared to warehouse-fresh Esskay, Gwaltney, Briggs, Smithfield, and Rapa; and warehouse-frozen Jimmy Dean and Jones Dairy.

H. G. Parks Inc. distribution locations were 284 Portsea Street New Haven, Connecticut; 319 North Preston Street, Philadelphia, Pennsylvania; and 533 Barretto Street, Bronx, New York. He also had locations in Somerset, New Jersey, and Providence, Rhode Island. It was Henry's desire to locate in North Carolina, Michigan, and Illinois to cover the southern region and the Midwest, but these plans never materialized.

In the state of Maryland, Parks Sausage was placed on sale in the postcommissary at the United States Army's Aberdeen Proving Ground. Parks Sausage was the first black firm to have its product accepted and sold on a United States installation.

This first step led to the product being sold at Fort Meade, Maryland; the United States Navy Station, Maryland; the United States Naval Academy, Maryland; the United States Navy Yard No. 29 in Philadelphia; McGuire Air Force Base, Philadelphia; Fort Dix, New Jersey; Fort Monmouth, New Jersey; Fort Wadsworth, New York; Walter Reed Army Center, Washington, DC; Andrews Air Force Base, Washington, DC; Bolling Air Force Base, Washington, DC; Fort McNair, Washington, DC; Cameron Station, Washington, DC; Fort Hamilton, New York; Fort Jay, New York; and Fort Myers, Virginia.

At the time, Henry thought this was unbelievable and never forgot how the United States military supported his business.

Henry was invited by Defense Supply Agency, Defense Personnel Support Center, Philadelphia, Pennsylvania, to address the management club on April 22, 1975. The management club consisted of over four hundred members from all levels of the agency who were seeking ways of developing their leadership and performance skills. Henry accepted this invitation with an open heart and felt this was the least he could do, considering all the military had done for H. G. Parks Inc.

Henry's address was entitled Minorities in the Future of Management. Henry spoke of the process of starting H. G. Parks Inc. He spoke of how he had been denied, he had been lied to, he had been pushed back but realized it was easy to be negative, possibly to hate and look back in anger but he said nothing is gained without a positive approach. He said that attitudes are changing about race around the world, and that "tomorrow's leaders are apt to be the sons and daughters of today's minority blue-collar workers." He further discussed an article from *Fortune* magazine, April 1975, where corporations were hiring minorities but few had risen to positions of real authority. He closed his address by directing the audience to get deeply involved in management; study it, practice it, and to prepare for upward mobility. He said that needs and changing times will make for openings.

Until Henry sold his shares in the company, H. G. Parks Inc. had never posted a losing year since 1951, the year H. G. Parks Inc. opened.

Publicity

I am a not a Negro businessman. I am a businessman who is Negro.
—Henry G. Parks Jr.

Henry G. Parks was everywhere. From Ohio to New York to Baltimore and Washington, DC, Henry was visible not only in the interest of his business but in public and private sectors doing good things for people, and publicity followed.

The *Journal Herald* series: "A casualty of desegregation? Negro youth studied hard in Dayton, Ohio. Henry G. Parks, Sr., 2519 Lakeview Avenue, retired employee of the Biltmore Hotel speaks of his son, 'was a boy who kept his head in the books a lot' during his growing up years in Dayton. After graduating from high school with honors he joined the Civilian Conservation Corp (CCC) and went to camp near Chillicothe. But the water was bad and the camp closed shortly after his arrival, his father recalled. Returning to Dayton he went to work in the kitchen of the Biltmore, at a job his father helped him obtain. After a year he went to Ohio State University where he again graduated with honors."

The *National Provisioner* reports the news, trends, innovation, and technical insights driving the meat, poultry, and seafood processing industries. On May 5, 1956, they reported in an article entitled "Opportunity's door is open to Enterprise" that "in five years a Baltimore producer of southern pork sausage and other unusual specialties captures a good market in eastern seaboard cities and builds an interesting new processing plant."

The *Jersey Journal* and the *Jersey Observer*, Monday, November 18, 1963: "Negro in business wants no advantage." The biography for this article begins, "Henry G. Parks, Jr., *the Negro president* of a Baltimore Maryland sausage . . ." This type of publicity would really get Henry annoyed. Henry would retort, "I am not a Negro businessman. I am a businessman who is Negro." The article further states that Henry wanted to sell his product competitively to all consumers regardless of race. Henry is described as "a new breed of Negro in business—the entrepreneur who has advanced out of the traditionally restricted Negro market to compete in what

Negro intellectuals like to call 'the American mainstream.' Though active in the civil rights movement, he carefully separates this activity from his business life. Says Parks 'this is business I'm in, not a social battle.'"

The article further states, "Parks Sausage has 140 employees, 80% of the consumers are white but most do not know that he is Negro. He advertises heavily and avoids the image of a Negro product. The advertisements 'More Parks' Sausages, Mom' made a great impact, the company has a few white salesmen and a few white production workers."

Henry states, "I have been insulted to the point of desperation, and I have swallowed gall. I have diverted my reaction, however, to positive purposes. I don't like to spend too much time contemplating on the past. I have gone into business, civic affairs, and politics without being resentful and negative . . . I did not think the big companies were ready to allow a Negro to advance . . . so I resigned and went into business myself."

In the United States Congressional Record, volume 109, number 199, of Friday, December 6, 1963: "The Negro businessman in America, Mr. Scott. Mr. President, recently a series of articles appeared in the *Harrisburg Patriot-News*. I believe they make a significant contribution to a much needed understanding of the problems and challenges faced by Negro Americans in the business world. I ask unanimous consent that the articles, written by Morton A. Reichek for Advance News Service, be printed in the Congressional Record. "There being no objection, the articles were ordered to be printed in the Congressional Record . . . Baltimore, Maryland, 'I am not a Negro businessman. I am a businessman who is Negro.'"

Bradford Jacobs, *Baltimore Sun*, wrote an editorial "Got to Get One." In his editorial about Mr. Parks, Mr. Jacobs pointed out how the federal government attempted to show goodwill to the African American community, offering Henry a post on a high-level government commission. At the time, the federal government did not have a good track record for recruiting and retaining African Americans in high government positions.

In the article by Mr. Jacobs, Henry asked the secretary of the federal office, "Mr. Secretary, tell me the truth. Why do you want to put a little man like me on a big, fancy commission like that?" A short silence, some muttering, then came the confession, "Look, Mr. Parks, we've got to get a, uh, Negro. Won't you do it?" The article further states that "Henry accepted the federal appointment. He was then called the Business Man's Negro, then a fashionable title among business man-collectors."

Henry is featured on the May 18, 1968, cover of *BusinessWeek*: "Baltimore businessman Henry G. Parks Jr., A Negro integrates his market." *BusinessWeek* is a McGraw-Hill publication. The story described the difficulties of a Negro owning a business: "The business owner has to be a soldier and a half. He runs in to trouble every step of the way. First, where does he get the money? Second, where can he locate his plant? Third, who will sell him his equipment and supplies? Fourth, where will he get his management and sales team? Fifth, will the people come when he is ready for business?"

Baltimore magazine, "Black capitalism: color it green," May 1970. This article features H. G. Parks Inc., Advanced Federal Savings and Loan Company, and Central Dodge as the three leading black-owned businesses in Baltimore. It is believed that Henry was the first to receive a loan by a Baltimore bank. These businesses could not compete with Black and Decker or Bethlehem Steel but were mainstreaming the American economy. Andrew Brimmer, then a member of the board of governors of the Federal Reserve's system and the most respected black professional in economic circles, received a push back when he made the statement "Encouraging black-owned businesses in city ghettos is a mistaken strategy for promoting racial equality." Brimmer insisted, "If many more black businesses are formed, they would certainly be prone to failure." The Baltimore Council for Equal Business Opportunity Inc. and outcries from other business and government leaders had a different view and challenged Mr. Brimmer's statement.

In the July 1972 issue of *Signature* magazine: "Mr. Parks' $10 Million Recipe, man on the move. Henry G. Parks Jr." Henry is described as a "doer" all his life, in fair and foul weather, earning for himself an enviable reputation. "He was born with his rich coloring, and, in the argot of the day, he is black. A black businessman, a successful black businessman." Even by this time in American history, Henry continued to be described as a "*black* businessman," rather than "a *businessman* who is black."

Henry once told a newspaper reporter, "I got used to being thrown out of places and then going back, and I guess I grew through adversity."

Training and Continued Learning

It is not the amount of education you have but the amount of it you use.
—Henry G. Parks Jr.

As much as Henry loved his business, he always found time for training and learning opportunities. He was both a teacher and a learner.

Throughout the years, Henry continued to learn state-of-the-art techniques to stay abreast of current trends, innovations, and technology associated with the manufacturing industry. He joined numerous professional groups and organizations to learn how to improve his performance. Through his memberships to various organizations, he affiliated with peers and those executives senior to him in business and industry. Henry was driven to self-improvement since exposure to the real insider information was not accessible to him.

As early as his completion of his bachelor's degree from Ohio State University in 1939, Henry continued graduate courses to further his knowledge in the fields of marketing, business, and commerce to achieve greater advantage.

In 1954, Henry completed trainings in Frontiers of America, Tidewater Chapter, at the Business Institute; and in 1957, Henry completed training at the University of Baltimore, School of Business, Industry, and Management, Management Clinic on executive thinking, planning, and action.

H. G. Parks Inc. was conferred a member of the American Meat Institute Foundation at the University of Chicago. The meat institute is a research and education foundation that recognizes the interest demonstrated in the application of science. This science is used for the development of information that leads to technological advances in the processing and utilization of products derived from livestock. Henry was recognized for his financial support used for scientific and technological research fields, which are conducted by the American Meat Institute Foundation at the University of Chicago, 1962-1963.

The Small Business Guidance and Development Center at Howard University, Washington, DC, developed a management brief from the content of a presentation Henry made to the center faculty. The brief is entitled "Successful Business Operation by Henry G. Parks Jr., president H. G. Parks Inc., Baltimore, Maryland." The brief is as relevant now as it was then. It reads:

> It is time that all of us begin to think of getting out of ghettoized activity; it is time we sought to enter into the main stream of business. I am not talking about becoming a general motor overnight, but I am talking about serving the needs of people wherever they are and establishing a business for that purpose.
>
> This country has a mandate to encourage small business. It is essential to the preservation of our whole economic system. We must make it popular to be in business or at least sympathetic to business. Many efforts are being made to encourage entrepreneurs. A man must always be able to rise if he is fortunate and smart enough to have the right sense of timing, if he has the required talent, and is willing to toil.
>
> In operating a successful business, we must continue to look at all practical and realistic growth possibilities. We should take a good look at franchising; we should take a good look at horizontal growth, such as expanding the number of markets; we should look at vertical growth, such as increasing the number of items or services that we are involved with. In operating a successful business we must grow at a rate that will enable us to get off the thin ice of a newly created small business or where the size and margin does not permit consistent profits or true organization.

At one time, we were our own package designers, advertising agency, lawyer and what have you. However, as we grow it is important that we know that the most successful business operator is the one who knows how to utilize talents of others. You get to the point that you dare not design a package without consulting a qualified package designer, that you go to an established advertising agency to make up your campaigns, that you seek the advice of lawyers on all legal matters. In doing all of this, it is absolutely necessary that while you receive all the advice and information you can afford, be certain that the final decision is yours own. You should determine to rise or fall on your own decision making, but that these decisions will be based upon the most up to date information you can get. Find additional ways of getting information by attending institutes, by subscribing to trade journals, by keeping up with current events, by skimming through information on business and economics, for it is truly helpful in setting the pace for your own activities.

It is important that you know how to conduct your affairs so as to establish financial responsibility. No business can grow without capital. Banks today are liberal in their help of a business that is promising and has someone who is a sound operator. Such things as paying bills promptly and taking advantage of appropriate discounts, of submitting statements and information that make sense to the credit agencies and to your bank. Giving off the atmosphere of commonsense and ability will go a long way towards getting favorable decisions when you apply for loans necessary to promote your business.

Involving yourself in community activities not only will give you a sense of participation and necessary knowledge as to what makes people tick, but it will add to the stature of your organization. Your public relations responsibilities are inside your own business, as well as in the community. Bite off only what you can chew, but I am certain part of operating a successful business is responsible participation in some community affairs.

We have discussed a number of factors that have to do with successful business operation. Not that throughout this brief that a thread persists. It is that nothing will beat common sense. It is not the amount of education and knowledge that you have, it is the amount that your use that counts. I have seen many instances where successful operators with little education and a whole lot of commonsense have become our greatest successes. I have seen people with doctorates fail through their inability to apply their knowledge in a common sense way. Being a part of a successful business operation is to me, one of the most exciting things that can happen. I hope you feel the same.

Henry was elected to the board of directors of the United States Chamber of Commerce on June 30, 1965. In 1971, Henry was an advisory board member of the National Alliance of Businessmen, an organization to foster job opportunities in the business sector for disadvantaged persons, needy youth, and for Vietnam-era veterans to enter meaningful and productive jobs—JOBS Campaign. Henry employed at H. G. Parks Inc. several ex-offenders to support this program and to give the youth a second chance in the workforce. In 1972, Henry was elected vice president of the board of directors, Chamber of Commerce of Metropolitan Baltimore.

Henry was invited to speak before the sales and marketing representatives of Coca-Cola at a behavioral and marketing seminar on March 23-26, 1971, in Atlanta, Georgia. The topic of his speech was "*the environment for selling in the '70s.*" Henry spoke from a small business perspective and his experiences as salesman. He spoke of developments in the marketing channels between retailer and the consumer. He said that too often, businesses feel that their overall or consumer-oriented advertising and promotion does the total job, but he said nothing replaces the value of salesmanship and sales promotion geared to the important public. That starts with the underside of the consumer and works back. As you sell in the '70s, you must be armed with the tools and resources to honestly answer or explain how we are facing the duality of objectives of making a better world while continuing to make a reasonable profit. He says that "we must be very concerned with minorities for they are not to be denied. Note that they are almost unanimous in their desires to join as full members of the American team. Our role to the consumer becomes fairly obvious so note again that it is important to differentiate between the customer and the consumer. Advertising must really be saying something. Aspirin may be aspirin but don't discount the healing value of a reassuring label." In closing, Henry stated, "Success in not obtained by declaration. It is the result of a smart practical plan, properly executed. Profits only come as the end result of having done the things right that contribute to profit."

On December 5, 1972, Henry led a seminar at the Massachusetts Institute of Technology (MIT) with Professor Frank Jones on "*how to get business and industry in to the Black community.*"

New Ventures

If race alone is not enough.
—Henry G. Parks Jr.

Although Henry was a success with H. G. Parks Inc., and the business was growing, he and Mr. Adams were always looking for new investment opportunities. With their combined knowledge, they had mastered the small-business game. If a business did not turn a reasonable profit, they knew to cut their losses and move on.

Henry, during this period, was attempting his hand at a new growth opportunity with Tuesday Publications. Formed in 1961, Tuesday was a Sunday news supplement to focus on the achievements of Negroes. It was an Illinois-based corporation of which Leonard Evans was editor and publisher. "*Look* and *Life*," said Mr. Evans, "are basically published for whites but also read by Negros. *Tuesday* is basically published for Negros and read by whites too." By February 1965, they moved from Illinois to Third Avenue in New York City.

Tuesday was placed every other month in nine major United States newspapers addressed primarily to whites: the *New York Journal-American*, the *Boston Sunday Advertiser*, the *Chicago Sun-Times*, the *Philadelphia Sunday Bulletin*, the *Detroit News*, the *Los Angeles Herald-Examiner*, the Cleveland *Plain Dealer*, the *Milwaukee Journal-Sentinel*, and the Rochester *Times-Union*.

Henry was elected to the board of directors of Tuesday and became vice president. In this role, he asked four of his Baltimore friends along with himself to invest $10,000 each in the publication, totaling $50,000 collectively. Venture capitalist, Mr. Adams, invested in the publication and was a member of the board of directors. On November 15, 1965, Henry and Mr. Adams, along with the three investors, signed a note and stock warrant agreement. They became stockholders in Tuesday.

In February 1965, Malcolm X was assassinated. Malcolm dated Henry's sister Jeanne briefly; he described Jeanne as the most beautiful woman he had ever seen in his book *The Autobiography of Malcolm X* as told to Alex Haley. Malcolm and Henry totally disagreed philosophically on race relations in the United States. Henry always felt responsible for his sister Jeanne's early death and believed Malcolm was associated with the death, but since the two were so different, it was never discussed. Tuesday was proceeding well with its newspaper supplement, and in January 1975, *Tuesday* magazine sponsored the Pro-Am Invitational Golf Tournament at the Grossinger's Hotel and Country Club, Grossinger, New York. Henry played in the tournament.

Approximately ten years after Henry and his Baltimore friends made the investment in *Tuesday* magazine, the publisher defaulted on the loan. The loan was made in Henry's and Mr. Adams's names. Eventually, the publication shut down. Henry and Mr. Adams were stuck with paying the entire $50,000 loan. He was angry and frustrated. While Henry and I were reviewing photographs for this project, I asked about a picture of a man who was unfamiliar to me. Henry looked at the picture and said, "I don't want to talk about it. That is the man from Tuesday who left town owing me money."

Henry had made agreements with honorable and reputable people. He was not familiar with businessmen who defaulted on loans and failed to honor their agreements. To breach an agreement is a breach of trust. Henry was deceived. He was very sensitive about this. He looked at me and said with disgust, "If race alone is not enough." He was ripped off by someone of his race.

In November 1966, Parks Motor Rentals Inc. was another business venture for Henry, and Mr. Adams was a silent partner. Parks Motor Rentals was a truck-leasing company. Available for rent were panel trucks to tractor-trailer rigs. This enterprise was a tax advantage at the time. In a few years, he was out of this business.

Henry invested in venture capital opportunities that provided new sources of revenue after selling his interest in H. G. Parks Inc. These ventures created safe and affordable housing for Baltimore City dwellers and senior citizens in minority communities such as Morrell Park senior citizens apartments, Lakeside Apartments, and Marlborough Apartments.

Unionized Employees

We realize that you voted not to have a union and then we turned around and asked you to accept the union.

—Henry G. Parks Jr.

By 1958, Henry voluntarily unionized H. G. Parks Inc. He foresaw the benefits of union protections. By making this decision, he knew he could avoid the negative attention of marches and protests and, most importantly, the time taken from producing the product. Henry ran a tight timeline.

H. G. Parks Inc. had established a substantial growth rate. Over twelve thousand stores were being serviced directly each week. The company had approximately 150 employees. Henry said, "I could not afford, not to get in front of this." From previous ventures, Henry was familiar with the threat of being close to losing everything. This was not worth the risk.

Henry called a meeting with his plant employees on November 22, 1958, at Wilson's Restaurant to acknowledge the signing of the union contract and to stress the importance of understanding its significance. In his speech, Henry stated,

> The union has sold us on the fact that employees deserve more consideration than any other factor in our organization . . . Let me point out that the company has made every effort to comply with request made by you . . . We realize that you voted not to have a union and then we turned around and asked you to accept the union . . . We want to walk into any situation without having to make any apologies. Our union is a good one. A good union, to me, is one that does the best for the employees while realizing that if the company can justify its existence the union must work with the company so it can stay in business . . . Our business can't stand still, unfortunately. We must grow . . . It means also, that in order for you to keep your job this company must go out and get more business . . . We all realize that if these goals are not obtained

there will be no business and consequently no jobs for any of us . . . We feel that because we are a small organization that we can become a close knit organization . . . Nothing will ever run completely smooth . . . This calls for tolerance. This calls for smart programming. This calls for handling problems before they become acute . . . Let's cooperate in making the relationship between labor and management one that will be a model for all others.

New Products

Something new and effective will be welcomed. Ideas?
—Henry G. Parks Jr.

In 1955, Henry added cooked chitterlings to his product line as a specialty product; just heat and eat. Henry's idea was to take chitterlings from a commonplace, low mark-up item, to a specialty. He thought the quality of his pork, flavored with spices from around the world, made it a premium product.

Henry believed poor people would not pay the price for this product. He thought wealthy people were too concerned with diet, thus his market was hardworking people—those who ate substantial foods would purchase this product. "These are our repeat customers." For those who responded negatively to this new product, he would say, "Something new and effective will be welcomed. Ideas?"

The H. G. Parks Inc. sausage line included pure pork sausage, smoked pork sausage, hot and "sagey," very hot and "sagey," beef sausage, brown and serve pork sausage, little linked sausage, and headcheese. Henry made history and gained a following by using odorless chitterlings in his sausage line, something never done before.

By 1957, Parks Sausage was trying its hand with frozen barbecue beef sandwich, foil wrapped. In July 1960, the company added the first smoked products. In May 1965, scrapple was added.

Phase II Expansion

If keeping it cool, keeping it clean and keeping it moving are the maxims for meat products they are doubly true for pork items.
—Henry G. Parks Jr.

Henry had ambitious plans to sell Parks Sausage products first to the southern region followed by the Midwest. Given that the Baltimore-Washington market spilled over into Northern Virginia, he looked to another southern state.

In my conversations with Henry, he stated that he had built and fully stocked a plant in the south. As soon as it was stocked, it was set on fire. When the investigation was completed, he asked why such an incident had occurred. He was told that the south did not want his "nigger sausages." Henry's reply was "My sausage is not made out of niggers!"

After purchasing four acres in Camden Industrial Park in Baltimore, the company opened a modern and efficient plant on April 1, 1967, closing the 2460 Woodbrook Avenue location, which he considered as his first expansion phase, from the rear of the Pennsylvania Avenue location. The new Parks Sausage plant was opened at 501 West Hamburg Street in Baltimore. The new plant was hailed a state-of-the-art facility by the meat manufacturing industry.

The plant received praise from health officials, who, on occasion, used the plant as a model to show how cleanliness in meat handling can be attained. The U-shaped processing area was environmentally controlled where meat products were manufactured. The shipping area and receiving departments were electronically controlled and designed to service ten thousand stores per week. A special feature of the plant was the twenty-one thousand square feet of individualized refrigerated areas with temperatures ranging from ten degrees below to forty-five degrees above zero. This eliminated the risk of highs and lows in temperature control—vital to the storage and processing of meat products. Henry stated, "If keeping it cool, keeping it clean and keeping it moving are the maxims for meat product they are doubly true for pork items." The plant had a research and development laboratory, executive offices, and employee areas—all were state of the art.

The plant was built by Henry A. Knott Inc., and Henschien, Everds, and Crombie were the architects. The plant was thirty thousand square feet on a 3.8-acre site bounded by Hamburg, Cross, Eutaw, and Russell Streets. This location was six blocks from downtown and near the north and south feeder lanes to the Baltimore-Washington Parkway. It was estimated that it would cut two hours off the travel to New York and to Boston. On a different side of the plant were the railroad tracks, which reduced the distance to the plant to just a few hundred feet. This made the pickup of loads of pork simple and perfect for maintaining temperatures. The plant was constructed at a cost of one million dollars. The company, at this point, had a six-million-dollar annual gross income and an estimated one-million-dollar annual payroll with 150 employees. In May of the same year, the Council for Equal Business Opportunity awarded H. G. Parks Inc. for this overwhelming expansion achievement.

For many years, Henry was unable to procure commercial funding for an expansion project. Henry was first denied due to race and, later, because of his association with Mr. Adams, his silent partner—who, according to the Baltimore banks, had a spot on his character for illegal activities. Due to Henry's consistent integrity, determination, high ethical standards, and his engagement in the affairs of the black community, he eventually was viewed on his own merits and not his association with Mr. Adams, and thus was offered loans.

Baltimore banks that had rejected him automatically in the past loaned him a million dollars to expand the Parks Sausage plant to the Baltimore Camden Yards, the present site of the Baltimore Stadium. The Maryland National Bank was the first to offer financing for construction of the property. The second loan came from Monumental Insurance Company for the mortgage.

On February 17, 1968, the Council for Equal Business Opportunity recognized Henry for distinguished growth through the development of a modern plant facility and outstanding business achievement by Benjamin Goldstein, director. Henry, by this point, had been honored beyond compare for numerous reasons up and down the Eastern Seaboard, but this appeared daunting to the black community. How did Henry do this after so many years of struggle? Many would have accepted defeat.

Three years later, in 1970, Henry announced the opening of two new distribution centers in Connecticut and New York and the proposed expansion of the Baltimore plant. Baltimore mayor, Thomas J. D'Alesandro III's administration introduced legislation to permit H. G. Parks Inc. to use the city's credit to borrow $1.37 million at 6 percent interest. This transaction was made possible by Maryland state law designed to assist Maryland subdivisions retain their industries and encourage expansion.

Stock Issue

If you don't owe anybody anything then you don't have to kiss their asses.
—Henry G. Parks Jr.

Henry made no bones about saying he did not like personal debt.

In January 1969, the company made its first public issue of stock. There were approximately 480,000 shares outstanding.

When Henry made a stock issue, it was to raise money for the company. As a result, he became highly visible in corporate America, calling attention to H. G. Parks Inc. Along with the United States Department of Agriculture approval for his meat products and conducting interstate commerce, H. G. Parks Inc. was on the map in corporate America. He acknowledged he was a small business relative to corporate America, but he felt the principles of growth and development were the same for both large and small businesses.

In June 1969, H. G. Parks Inc. became the first black-owned company to trade on Wall Street. This was the same year and month of the Stonewall riot, marking the beginning of the gay rights movement. When interviewing Henry on this coincidence, he offered no comment but a big smile. I laughed out loud.

Selling H. G. Parks Inc. to the Norin Corporation

Haysbert is going to sink the company.

—H. G. Parks Jr.

One evening while I was visiting Henry at his home in Bolton Hill, he asked me, prior to selling H. G. Parks Inc., if I thought he should sell the company. I appreciated his asking me the question, but I never understood why he thought I could answer his question. I was aware that, in his mind, if I were properly trained, I could run the company, but I never gave that a thought. I also knew he would never beg anyone for anything. If you did not show keen interest up front for him to discern and notice, he would not suggest it.

Henry was haggard and tired from years of thinking and negotiating how to best dispose of his company. He had so hoped over the years that someone young and black would take interest in learning and running his company. He had hired a young black Harvard graduate whom I thought he had hoped would take over the company. Henry had served on the Urban National Corporation and was exposed to Ivy Leaguers, but no one seemed to be interested in running a pork manufacturing plant.

Henry could see the uncertainty on my face because I was thinking, *I don't know how to run a manufacturing plant,* but I did not want to put a voice to it.

"What a tough decision, I thought". With all his success in business and politics, he had never considered that someday he would need to transition the company. He said to me, "I need fifteen more years."

I replied yes to his question "Should I sell the company?" I had watched for a long time how Henry tried to stop and conceal tremors of his advancing Parkinson's disease. In my opinion, I saw no sense in exacerbating the disease by continuing to remain in a stressful work environment to save any business. Henry's health was more important and a more sensible decision in my thinking. I knew too that in Henry's soul, it was like cutting off three-quarters of his body for me to tell him yes. He wanted an answer that I could not provide.

On April 10, 1977, the *New York Times* wrote an article on the sale of Henry's 153,000 shares of stock to the Norin Corporation of Miami for $1.58 million. Norin Corporation's primary products were in life, fire, and casualty insurance. Henry got a seven-year contract and remained the chairman of the board of H. G. Parks Inc. and served on the board of Norin as a consultant. Raymond S. Haysbert became president and chief executive officer.

Mr. Haysbert was a professor of business administration at Wilberforce University in Ohio before joining H. G. Parks Inc. Henry and Mr. Haysbert were longtime friends since their days in Ohio.

Norin also bought 153,000 shares from William Adams, his silent partner.

Henry said he was looking for a growth pattern when he sold to Norin. Norin offered $10 a share for the stock. It was the highest offer, and that seemed to be the best solution for Henry and Mr. Adams, but Mr. Haysbert was not pleased. He was thinking he was heir apparent after so many years of being general manager.

Henry sold H. G. Parks Inc. because the company was at the height of its production capacity, but moreover, he was diagnosed three years earlier with Parkinson's disease. Henry knew that he could not go on managing the company. He had also watched his mother, who he dearly loved, deteriorate from the same disease.

The regional competitor at this time was Habbersett Brothers of Philadelphia; nationally was Jones Dairy Farm of Fort Atkinson in Wisconsin, Bob Evans of Ohio, Jimmy Dean of Texas, and Gwaltney of Smithfield, Virginia.

In 1979, the Norin Corporations sold H. G. Parks Inc. to Cannellus Inc., a subsidiary of Canadian Pacific Corporation that had plans to liquidate. However, a group of Parks employees, led by Mr. Haysbert, bought the company back with a leveraged buyout and the help of city financing in 1980. Henry thought the move very unwise and was totally distraught. Henry would have preferred the company be cleanly liquidated than to see his former employee make such an unwise move and lose money.

When Henry and I visited again, I asked, "What is wrong with you?" He paused and simply said, "Haysbert is going to sink the company." Henry thought the leveraged buyout was not sound, but he stuck with Mr. Haysbert's decision and remained the chairman of the board. The company struggled.

In 1987, Sara Lee bought 45 percent of the company, but 55 percent of the company was black-owned. Mr. Haysbert and his son owned 51 percent of the company. On September 29, 1987, Henry's birthday, he resigned as chair of the board and member of the board of directors.

Henry introduced me to Mr. Haysbert for the purposes of conducting an interview for this book. Mr. Haysbert, as well as Henry's secretary, was fully familiar with me. I have no idea what Henry told them about me, but they provided me with everything I needed. Henry's secretary said, "You are a lucky person, Maurice, because Henry does not trust very many people."

In the interview with Mr. Haysbert, I learned he joined H. G. Parks Inc. in 1952. He was one of the owners of the Forum Caterers of Baltimore. He was more than willing to conduct the interview and agreed to my recording his conversation. We met in Mr. Haysbert's office, formerly occupied by Henry. Henry left us alone to talk. He was very enthusiastic and talkative about the Parks-Haysbert relationship. Mr. Haysbert was a good sport with me during the interview process. Mr. Haysbert went all the way back to Henry's college days and told stories as to how Henry got started in the sausage business, and provided names and addresses of other individuals who could contribute to this biography.

He followed up our interview with a letter to me stating how fortunate Henry was to have started on his biography.

Henry respected Mr. Haysbert well enough but did not agree with the wraparound debt Mr. Haysbert used to buy back the company. Henry did not believe this was a good business decision.

Henry was right.

The company filed for bankruptcy protection in 1996 and eventually changed hands again.

CHAPTER 2

Corporate America

Obviously, I cannot send a passport by January 24 [1969]
since I have never obtained one.
—Henry G. Parks Jr.

While running the H. G. Parks Inc. and after issuing H. G. Parks Inc. stock on the New York Stock Exchange, Henry became widely recognized and respected by corporate America. His election to the First Pennsylvania Bank Corporation in 1971 led to his election to the board of directors of the Magnavox Company; VNC Ventures, formerly the Urban National Corporation; W. R. Grace & Company; First Pennsylvania Bank NA; Signal Corporation; Warner-Lambert; and First Pennsylvania Financial Services. Simultaneously, he was relentlessly engaged in the support of national organizations like the United Negro College Fund, the National Urban League, the National Association for the Advancement of Colored People, and the Greater Baltimore Committee.

Henry was invited by *Time* magazine to take the *Time* Life Tour to Southeast Asia that departed the United States on February 20, 1969. It was during the preparation for this tour that Henry was asked to send his passport to *Time* magazine. In a letter dated January 17, 1969, Henry replied, "Obviously, I cannot send a passport by January 24th since I have never obtained one." In the process of applying for his passport, he needed a birth certificate. When he applied for the birth certificate and it was returned, he remembered that he was born Henry Faris Parks and not Henry Green Parks Jr., so he needed to correct his name.

On February 14, 1969, Henry sent an all-company bulletin to inform employees that he had accepted an invitation from Time Inc. to join a group of business leaders on a news tour of Southeast Asia. Time Inc., publishers of *Time*, *Life*, and *Fortune* magazines, had made advanced program arrangements for the group to meet with top political, economic, and military figures in the places to be visited. The destinations included Honolulu, Manila, Saigon, Bangkok, Kuala Lumpur, Singapore, Jakarta, Seoul, Kyoto, and Tokyo. Henry explained the trip would not only be used as a sound public relations matter but an opportunity to increase insight as to what is going on in the places around the world that were making news headlines.

Prior to departure, news tour participants met in the Dolly Madison Room at the Madison Hotel, Washington, DC, on March 11, and later in the afternoon, met with President Richard M. Nixon at the White House.

Henry had a great time on the tour to Southeast Asia. Upon his return, he wrote a letter on March 17, 1969, to James A. Linen, president of *Time* magazine stating,

> By all standards my invite was unusual and my acceptance was unique. In spite of my positive actions, I've had a "thing" about big business and its denials to my people. The tour is making me think deeper and broader and such reaffirms my conclusion that it is the system, not the individual people. It's absolutely amazing in this computerized age how much still depends, at the very top levels, on the right man at the right time. And how important it is for people to meet and really get to know each other. My participation is a tiny part of many "beginnings."

In 1972, William Boucher III, director of the Greater Baltimore Committee, described Henry in this way: "He's an important bridge between business and government; he personifies that partnership. He also bridges the black and white communities here, and that's awfully important in an area that is about 50-50 black and white."

On January 17, 1975, Henry was invited by publisher Ralph P. Davidson to take the *Time* magazine Middle East news tour. In a letter from the publisher of *Time*, dated February 10, 1975, the article highlighted the tour stating that the news tour, made up of United States businessmen, journalists, and others, found themselves the subjects of kings, emirs, prime ministers, and presidents. The tour was two weeks, and they visited eleven nations. The tour represented collectively one and one-half million people and had 1974 sales of nearly $100 billion. The tour provided an opportunity for business leaders to pose hard questions to heads of state on oil and investment policy, petrodollar recycling, and the prospects for war or peace. This was the seventh tour. Henry was invited to participate in the first tour in 1969.

In planning a tour to Africa, Henry wrote a letter to Ralph P. Davidson on November 19, 1976, recommending the names of Ben Hooks as he moved from the Federal Communications Commission to take over the NAACP from Roy Wilkins, who was retiring; Congressman Andrew Young; Congresswoman Barbara Jordan; and Bill Coleman, secretary of transportation. Henry stated, "The thing that is significant is that the minority community is coming up with good performers."

During Henry's corporate-America years, he could no longer travel solo or with his daughters to many corporate events. He needed a wife. And thus he made an agreement with Alice Gwathney Pinderhughes—after her husband had died in 1972—to be his friend and companion. I thought Alice was perfect. Henry, Alice, and I were great friends and occasionally socialized together.

Henry took Alice all over the world as friend and companion to corporate events. Alice was treated first class and received the red carpet treatment. They were a very nice team. This was a relationship similar to Governor William Donald Schaefer and his childhood friend Hilda Mae Snoops.

Henry and Alice did not share the same quarters when they traveled. Alice presented herself faithfully and loyally to Henry as she was. Alice was educated, a professional career woman, and possessed the grace and dignity of a fine lady. Alice was received by the CEOs and their wives without question.

Alice grew up in the small Green Spring Valley community of Chattolanee in Baltimore County. She was an only child of James Hugh and Rebecca Gwathney. Her father was a butler, and her mother did not work. As a child, she played with wealthy white children on the estate where her father worked. The estate was later passed down to the Gwathney family. Her father was buried in a plot on the estate. Alice, like Henry, loved to read. This was a common ground for both of them.

Living on a posh estate, Alice could not debut with her white friends nor could she attend their schools. She moved to the city and graduated from Douglass High School. She received a teaching certificate from Coppin State University and took numerous graduate courses but never earned a master's degree.

In 1943, she started her career in education at the Gilmore Elementary School as a teacher. She worked in many roles before becoming assistant superintendent for elementary education.

When William Donald Schaefer was mayor, he convinced the school board to elevate Alice to Baltimore City School superintendent. She was openly and harshly criticized for not having a terminal degree in that the mission of education was to promote advanced role models. She never reminded her critics that blacks were barred from graduate programs at the University of Maryland until after the United States Supreme Court *Brown v. the Board of Education* decision in 1954.

Alice was the city's first woman superintendent. She was credited with restoring the school system's creditability in the business community. I was employed by the Baltimore City school system as well. Henry never said, but I thought he was instrumental in Mayor Schaefer's nomination of Alice for the post. This post gave Alice the status and prestige while she accompanied Henry in corporate America.

Mayor Kurt L. Schmoke asked her to retire in late 1987. The Baltimore old guard, white and black, did not like this decision and undermined the mayor.

First Pennsylvania Corporation

Quite frankly, we were aghast that he wasn't already on some Baltimore
bank board. When we found out, we rushed to get him.

—John R. Bunting

In 1971, Henry was appointed to the board of directors of the First Pennsylvania Corporation. Henry served on the audit and trust audit committees. First Pennsylvania Corporation was a bank holding company that owned all the stock of First Pennsylvania Bank NA. The bank, which was the corporation's only major subsidiary, was engaged in the commercial banking and trust business. It conducted such business in regional, national, and international markets from its Philadelphia headquarters and from other domestic and foreign offices, including sixty-seven branches in southeastern Pennsylvania.

This was the first board to which Henry was elected. John R. Bunting was chairman. Mr. Bunting was mindful of Henry's standing in the business community but was more mindful of his standing in the Negro community. Mr. Parks's race was the major thing that they were after. "Quite frankly, we were aghast that he wasn't already on some Baltimore bank board. When we found out, we rushed to get him," Mr. Bunting added. Mr. Bunting recalled a board meeting where Henry listened carefully to a detailed report that had been prepared on the number of Negroes that worked at varying levels within the bank. Mr. Bunting said, "This study wouldn't have been made without Mr. Parks on the board . . . When it was over, Henry expressed interest in finding out what the Negro employment picture was in some of our other, nonbank holdings."

Henry was chairman of the 1972 Baltimore Corporate Campaign for the United Negro College Fund Inc. The First Pennsylvania Corporation sent a stock certificate for forty shares of First Pennsylvania Corporation stock made out to the United Negro College Fund. This stock was paid substantial dividends and was listed on the New York Stock Exchange.

Henry served on the First Pennsylvania board of directors for twelve years and was senior director. He received the First Pennsylvania Corporation service Award in 1983. The inscription on his award stated, "During his dozen years of service he demonstrated constant support and commitment to the corporation and gave it full benefit of his executive business experience integrity and professionalism. He gave valuable advice to management and the board concerning the creation and implementation of First Pennsylvania's outstanding affirmative action programs. His initiatives will provide for continued progress and future direction in the areas of corporate responsibility, signed: George A. Butler, Chairman and President."

Magnavox Company

He makes sure that we are doing what's right.
—Robert Platt

Three weeks after his election to the First Pennsylvania Corporation, Magnavox Company elected Henry to their board of directors. Henry was known on the board for selecting and promoting minority employment in the company.

Robert Platt was president and had met Henry in 1969 and persuaded him to become a board member. Mr. Platt explained it like this: "We're a consumer-oriented company. I said to him, 'We can use your special perspective . . . We can use help.' He makes sure that we are doing what's right. He helps us police ourselves."

In the September 25 issue of the *New York Observer* in 1971, Henry was honored for promoting minority employment. Henry also served on the audit committee of the board.

Henry served on the board of directors of Magnavox from 1971 to 1974.

Urban National Corporation / VNC Ventures

I am proud of my years connected with Urban National Corporation.
—Henry G. Parks, Jr.

Henry was elected to the board of directors for Urban National Corporation. He also served on the executive committee. Urban National Corporation is a private venture capital company started in 1971. The Urban National Corporation invests in developing companies with high growth potential. Their name changed in 1984 to VNC Ventures and, in 1979, moved to State Street, Boston, Massachusetts.

During this period in Boston's history, the city was experiencing unrest. In June of 1975, Judge Arthur Garrity issued a plan to desegregate Boston's public schools, ordering the busing of twenty-one thousand students. In response, race riots erupted in high schools in Hyde Park, Roxbury, and South Boston. Governor Francis Sargent called in the National Guard and appealed to President Ford to send federal troops to quell the disturbances. The violence in Boston represented the height of national tension over busing.

Investments made by VNC are limited to minority persons, including African Americans, Puerto Ricans, Mexican Americans, Native Americans, and members of other minority groups experiencing economic discrimination. Edward Dugger III is the president and CEO, a graduate of Harvard College and Princeton.

Henry was indeed honored to work with the young and talented minority lead corporation.

In 1980, Henry was on the board of directors of W. R. Grace & Company Inc. Via a letter dated July 8, Henry built bridges between W. R. Grace & Company Inc.—an old and well-established white-owned company, and VNC—a newly established minority-owned company, in hopes of integration of ideas, corporate collaboration, and future joint partnerships.

In a letter dated June 12, 1980, Henry built bridges between VNC and Azurdata of Washington State. Azurdata was interested in the sale of route accounting terminals of Entenmann's Bakery. Connecting the dots between different business sectors was something Henry engaged in frequently.

In a letter to Edward Dugger III, he stated he was proud of his years connected with VNC Ventures.

W. R. Grace & Company Inc.

This makes H. G. Parks, Inc. a small company. When you travel in these circles it makes you know the distance blacks must go.

—Henry G. Parks Jr.

In 1974, Henry was elected to the board of directors of W. R. Grace & Company Inc., a chemical and natural resources firm with retail and restaurant holding. Henry was chair of the committee on corporate responsibility. This was the year President Richard M. Nixon resigned and was replaced by Gerald Ford.

According to the *Baltimore Sun*, Sunday, December 14, 1980, W. R. Grace & Company was America's seventy-sixth most profitable public corporation, located at Grace Plaza, 114 Avenue of Americas, New York. The company had more than sixty thousand employees worldwide, just over 1,400 of them in Maryland. In 1979, the Grace & Company had $5.27 billion in sales and forecasted sales would surpass $6 billion in 1980.

In discussing the article with Henry, he said to me, "This makes H. G. Parks, Inc. a small company. When you travel in these circles it makes you know the distance blacks must go."

Different from Henry, J. Peter Grace was an old-line New York democrat; his grandfather was former mayor of the city. He grew up in Irish Catholic wealth and received the company from his father in 1945 at age thirty-two. This kind of pedigree makes a difference as to where a man or woman starts and ends in a race. Henry worked with Mr. Grace, and they became good friends. They called each other on a first-name basis. Henry was never intimidated by Mr. Grace and was proud of his accomplishments at H. G. Parks Inc. and remained positive.

Henry served on the dinner committee to support Felix E. Larkin, chairman of the board of W. R. Grace & Company, who received the National Brotherhood Award at the National Conference of Christians and Jews. The presentation was made on October 2, 1980, in the grand ballroom at the Pierre Hotel, New York.

It was the policy of W. R. Grace & Company to be responsible corporate citizens in any country in which they operated. Henry had an interest in the apartheid. As a result of negative press, Henry recommended that W. R. Grace & Company, who had holding there, consider its positions on apartheid carefully.

Due to Henry's influence, W. R. Grace & Company Inc. was a huge supporter of the Baltimore Arena Players, a theater group.

On February 10, 1989, Henry's daughter Grace sent a letter of resignation for her father from the W. R. Grace & Company after fifteen years. Henry commuted to and from New York for regular board meetings, across the United States, and around the world, striving to change the mentality of corporate America on the image of African Americans in the corporate boardroom.

First Pennsylvania Bank NA

When it was over, Henry expressed interest in finding out what the
Negro employment picture was in some of our other, non-bank holdings.
—John R. Bunting

Henry was elected to the board of directors of the First Pennsylvania Bank NA, 1975. He served on the trust audit committee. The committee coordinated audits of the fiduciary activities of the bank at least once during each calendar year and within fifteen months of the last audit, and at such other time or times as in its discretion seemed advisable. It also determined whether the fiduciary activities of the bank were administered in accordance with law and sound fiduciary principles.

Signal Companies

This was an opportunity to inform, guide, and ultimately bring
positive change to corporate policies.
—H. G. Parks Jr.

Henry was elected to the board of directors of the Signal Companies in 1976. He was initially assigned to work with the affirmative action team. By 1979, Henry worked with the stock option committee and the executive compensation committees for the corporation.

Henry flew to Scottsdale, Arizona, for the Affirmative Action Conference for all the Signal Companies including Mack Trucks Inc., the Garrett Corporation, and UOP Inc. The attendees were chief personnel executives and affirmative action officers. The meeting was designed to review the company's affirmative action progress since the last meeting, to look at future plans, and to look at the summer minority hiring programs. Henry listened to the reports and provided recommendations. He learned he was the right person to communicate with this group, mixed with liberals and conservatives without hostility. While listening to the reports, he could feel decades of past injustices to people of color. Henry's positive approach and attitude toward the problems enabled him to communicate effectively while holding his temper. "This was an opportunity to inform, guide, and ultimately bring positive change to corporate policies." It was clear to Henry that top management had no understanding of the plight of minorities but wanted fairness and equality but did not know how to proceed. They wanted his help.

Forrest N. Shumway, president, and his wife Patsy became good friends with Henry Parks and Henry's friend Alice Pinderhughes.

Warner-Lambert Company

Warner-Lambert pledge of one million dollars to the
United Negro College Fund.

—Joseph D. Williams

Warner-Lambert was a major multinational company serving the health and well-being of people around the world. Warner-Lambert products were marketed in more than 130 countries. The company employed approximately forty-two thousand people, operated more than one hundred manufacturing facilities, and maintained four major research centers. The largest portion of the company's business related to health care.

Other health-care products included nonprescription pharmaceuticals and personal care products. Warner-Lambert also was a major producer and marketer of chewing gums, breathe mints, shaving products, and pet care items.

Henry was elected to the Warner-Lambert board of directors in 1977. Henry served on the audit, corporate public policy, and retirement and savings plan committees.

Warner-Lambert hosted its annual meeting in Freiburg, Germany, on June 22-24, 1985. Joseph P. Williams was CEO. Henry and his friend Alice Pinderhughes attended and were guests at the Hotel Columbi.

Joseph D. Williams sent letters to Warner-Lambert board members on June 10, 1986, regarding the upcoming board meeting in Puerto Rico, held May 22, to

May 25, 1986. In his letter to Henry, he said it was great to be with Alice at the last meeting. Henry and Alice attended and were guests at the Hyatt Dorado Beach Hotel, Dorado, Puerto Rico.

In July 1986, Warner-Lambert contributed to the Bishop Tutu's Scholarship Fund for South African refugees.

Mr. Williams, chairman of Warner-Lambert, informed Henry of "Warner-Lambert's pledge of one million dollars to the United Negro College Fund." RJR Nabisco made a similar pledge.

Henry served on the Warner-Lambert Company board of directors for ten years.

CHAPTER 3

Public Servant

Henry Parks was a really solid stable voice for the black community in what was a turbulent period. His was a voice of reason that was respected and listened to by all the council members, and he was able to influence proper actions that might have been much more difficult to obtain had he not served.

—Thomas J. D'Alesandro III

Elected to the Baltimore City Council, Fourth District

In 1960, John F. Kennedy was elected president of the United States. Henry was happy with the outcome of the election. When I visited his office in Camden Yards approximately fifteen years later, a bust of the president was proudly displayed on his credenza along with voluminous other honors, awards, and recognitions from both the private and public sectors.

Well after Henry established H. G. Parks Inc., he was elected to public service. Baltimore City leaders were aware of Henry's commitment to the black community and his connection to the black networks, such as the Urban League, NAACP, and the United Negro College Fund. The city needed his help to resolve growing problems between blacks and whites not only in Baltimore but throughout the nation.

In January 1963, George Wallace, at his inauguration as governor of the state of Alabama, stated, "In the name of the greatest people that have ever trod this earth, I draw the line in the dust and toss the gauntlet before the feet of tyranny . . . and I say . . . segregation now! Segregation tomorrow! Segregation forever!"

In April, civil rights protesters led by Martin Luther King Jr. began boycotts, sit-ins, and demonstrations in Birmingham. Birmingham protesters were dispersed by police dogs in a violent scene that is televised today. King was arrested and jailed. While in jail, he issued his famous letter explaining why civil disobedience is justified.

Henry was elected, in 1963, to the Baltimore City Council, fourth district. He defeated Max Alpert, then president of the Trenton Democratic Club.

He was elected for two four-year terms. Henry received the Distinguished Citizen Citation as a distinguished citizen, successful businessman, and newly elected representative to the City Council of Baltimore on June 15, 1963.

In August 1963, 250,000 demonstrators participated in the March on Washington for jobs and freedom. Gathered at the Lincoln Memorial, Martin Luther King Jr. delivered his "I Have a Dream" speech. In November 1963, President John Fitzgerald Kennedy was assassinated in Dallas, Texas. Vice President Lyndon Baines Johnson became president.

Henry was effective as city councilman. He was aggressive and fearless and urged the Baltimore City Council in passing bills addressing issues of fair housing, public accommodations, and equal employment opportunity for black communities. He also was associated with the Metropolitan Transit Authority. Many voters had hopes that Henry would become Baltimore's first black mayor. He was able to consolidate the black communities and not alienate the white communities.

William Donald Schaefer stated, "He was a man of great vision, especially in the area of race relations."

In August 1963, Henry was appointed by J. Millard Taws, governor of the state of Maryland, to the Maryland Commission at the New York World's Fair in 1964-1965.

On November 24, 1964, Henry gave a speech to the Greater Baltimore Conference on Equal Opportunity in Housing at the Sheraton-Belvedere Hotel in the morning workshop. Henry stated at the workshop, "As the civil rights movement progresses in this country the housing question emerges as key issue. It reaches deep into the family, the true basis of our entire society. It has been said that we cannot legislate love. But it has been demonstrated that with the tool of legislation we can erect mighty barriers to hate and frustration and its consequences, and set a climate that can result in tolerance and understanding."

Henry was reelected for his second term as Baltimore City councilman on November 16, 1967. Thomas J. D'Alesandro III was mayor. Henry's term would expire December 9, 1971. He resigned a year early.

On May 25, 1967, Spiro T. Agnew, governor of the state of Maryland, conferred upon Henry a Certificate of Distinguished Citizenship for his outstanding and unique contributions to a total community as a councilman and for the City of Baltimore, and as a businessman, demonstrating integrity and ability and meriting trust and respect.

In the meantime, in 1967, President Johnson nominated Thurgood Marshall to the Supreme Court, becoming the first African American Justice of the

Supreme Court. Race riots erupted in cities across the country, including Chicago, Cleveland, Detroit, Memphis, Milwaukee, and Newark. President Johnson called on Henry to promote civil rights in all his travels.

It took four more years of fight before Congress passed the Civil Rights Act of 1968. President Johnson signed the act, making it unlawful to refuse to sell, rent, or negotiate for the sale or rental of a dwelling because of race or religion.

It was reported in the *Labor Herald* during this period that Councilman John Pica, 3rd District of Baltimore who led the fight in the Council against open housing, (an issue Henry was fighting for) was rushed to a local hospital for emergency treatment. The only bed available was in the ward. When he awoke, nine Negros were his roommates. I thought there was some sort of victory here.

In April 1968, Reverend Dr. Martin Luther King was assassinated and riots broke out across the United States in cities. In June, Robert F. Kennedy was assassinated.

In November 1968, Richard Nixon won the presidency. As president, Mr. Nixon shifted the emphasis away from the cutting off of federal funds to coerce desegregation and toward Justice Department—sponsored lawsuits. Throughout his presidency, Nixon repeatedly attacked busing and stated that he will do no more than the minimum required by law. On June 30, 1969, Maryland State Governor Marvin Mandel nominated and appointed Henry as a board member of the Metropolitan Transit Authority to work on issues of busing within the state of Maryland. The term ended July 1, 1972.

In one of our conversations, Henry shared with me that his decision to run for public office was, in retrospect, a mistake. He said it took too much time from his business. During his tenure on the council, he was accused of voting on issues that could advance H. G. Parks Inc. and thus implied a conflict of interest. Henry was livid and outraged by the accusation. He was more outraged, he said, because the allegation came from a black. Rather than create a nasty disagreement that would eventually become public, he chose to resign from the council one year prior to the end of his second term. It gave Henry comfort to say, "Maurice, I am a businessman first."

After Henry resigned from the city council, the city leadership continued to support him. In 1972, Thomas J. D'Alesandro III, former mayor, stated, "Henry Parks is a real good ambassador. As far as this city is concerned, the fact that he was there [on the city council in 1964] made it possible to get along. He could and did understand, interpret and explain legislation."

Herbert G. Bailey, executive director of the Baltimore Chamber of Commerce who worked for ten years on the Voluntary Council for Equal Opportunity, said, "Henry Parks is an impatient man in the most constructive sense of the word. He's impatient to get something done and not just sit there and talk about it. He has real influence at the state capital. Our governor pays a lot of attention to Henry."

Former mayor Thomas J. D'Alesandro III said, "Henry Parks was a really solid stable voice for the black community in what was a turbulent period. His was a voice of reason that was respected and listened to by all the council members, and he was able to influence proper actions that might have been much more difficult to obtain had he not served."

William Donald Schaefer, mayor of Baltimore City, issued a proclamation designating "Henry Parks Jr. Day in Baltimore, May 18, 1977" for outstanding contributions to the economic, social, and civic welfare of the city, distinguishing himself as one of the city's most respected business leaders; having started with two employees and an abandoned dairy building to make "More Parks' Sausages, Mom, Please!" a household phrase in the city that now markets along the East Coast; demonstrating faith in the city while providing numerous jobs to our residents; serving as former Baltimore City Council civil rights advocate, earning positions with the National Interracial Council for Business Opportunity and the Opportunities Industrial Center; being a life member of the NAACP and active fund-raiser for the United Negro College Fund to insure that young people of whatever race are not frustrated in their attempts to succeed.

Appointed President of the Board
of Fire Commissioner for the City of Baltimore

I think I have proved that black businessmen not only can be
successful but that they can be successful in the same terms as anybody else.
—Henry G. Parks Jr.

Eleven years after resigning from the Baltimore City Council and three years after selling his interest in the H. G. Parks Inc., Maryland Governor Harry Hughes invited Henry to be a part of the Maryland delegation visiting the People's Republic of China in 1980. The primary purpose of the exchange was to establish potential economic and trade development ties with the state. Ronald Reagan was elected president.

On March 11, 1981, Henry was appointed president of the Board of Fire Commissioners for the City of Baltimore by Mayor William Donald Schaefer. Henry was the first black to hold this position. Henry said, "I think I have proved that black businessmen not only can be successful but that they can be successful in the same terms as anybody else."

At the Board of Fire Commissioners meeting on December 22, 1982, the Vulcan Blazers Inc. complained about the disproportionately low percentages of blacks promoted to junior management, lieutenant, captain, and battalion chiefs within the fire department.

The *Baltimore Sun* banner line of November 16, 1983, stated "Fire Board Alters Policy on promotion . . . aim is to give blacks more high-level jobs." The City Board of Fire Commissioners announced changes in the promotion practices in an effort to elevate blacks to more responsible positions in the department. The decision meant the board would select from the top five persons on a promotional list, instead of selecting the first person on the list.

Henry explained the change was "appropriate for promoting minority persons without upsetting the apple cart" in an otherwise efficient fire department. Henry stated, "It has become important to bring the department's hierarchy in line with the nature of the community," pointing out the city has a black population of 50 percent while only 20 percent of the fire personnel were black.

The move was viewed critically by an official of the fire officers' union, who believed the traditional method of selection of the candidate was fairer. Henry's reply to the officer was "I'm not averse to doing things for affirmative action, but we've got to watch for reverse discrimination. We are walking a tightrope." Mayor William Donald Schaefer supported the fire department's affirmative action report and expressed hopes of making the fire department a true equal-opportunity employer.

Overall, black representation during Henry's tenure as president increased from 12 percent to 20 percent. Some firefighters were pleased with this statistic and others were not; they felt more could be done, but Henry publicly stated, "It will be business as usual if I remain in good health." He continued to work with the Vulcan Blazers Inc. over the years and was eventually praised and received accolades for his role in increasing job opportunities for blacks. Henry served as president of the Board of Fire Commissioners for seven years and resigned effectively, December 31, 1987.

In 1986, the black community supported William Donald Schaefer as governor. In January, a group of prominent black leaders met at the Omni Hotel in Baltimore to organize and strategize how the state was going to carry out plans to support Mr. Schaefer.

Henry had served as a member of the executive committee and treasurer of the Maryland Democratic State Central Committee. He also provided a liaison between the citizens of Baltimore, and the reelection committee for Mayor William Donald Schaefer.

Henry, William Adams, Sam Daniels, George Russell, and Otis Warren, along with other representatives from Harford County, Howard County, the Eastern Shore, and Baltimore City attended this meeting. The *Baltimore Sun Papers*, on April 3, 1986, printed "Black clerics, activists urge Schaefer to run for governor."

The *Baltimore Sun Papers* also printed on July 18, 1986, a highlighted letter from Sam Daniels, "Blacks United for Schaefer." Mr. Schaefer's accomplishments that supported the black community were his appointments of the first black police commissioner, the first black school superintendent, a black personnel director, and more. A press release "Citizens for Schaefer" and campaign schedule was August 1 to 31, 1986. There was a blacks-united-for-Schaefer motorcade and a rally itinerary at Schaefer headquarters, 1529 E North Avenue. Henry was adviser along with Willie Adams, George Russell, Sam Daniels, and Senator Clarence Blount.

William Donald Schaefer, a democrat, had one of the longest runs in American politics. After sixteen years as a city councilman, he won four terms as mayor (1971 to 1987), two terms as governor (1987 to 1995), and two terms as state comptroller (1999 to 2007). He was defeated in a 2006 bid for reelection; it was his first defeat in more than a half century.

After Henry's death in 1989, Congressman Paul Sarbanes recognized Henry posthumously in the Congressional Record—Wednesday, December 8, 1992— as black businessman of the year in the hall of fame. Henry was honored by the Baltimore Marketing Association; Ackneil M. Muldrow II, president; and William Donald Schaefer, who was Henry's dear friend.

CHAPTER 4

Giving Back

I think we need to learn how to be managers and how to operate profitable businesses, because we will never learn how to be strong as a people until we begin to have some self-sufficiency, to own, to have access to the money and the proper use of it.

—Henry G. Parks Jr.

National Urban League Inc.

The National Urban League was founded in 1910 in New York City. Henry was a continuous member of the National Urban League as a volunteer since 1935. The National Urban League is a professional community service organization created to secure equal opportunity for Negroes and other minorities. It is nonpartisan and interracial in its leadership and staff and seeks to foster good race relations and increased understanding among people. It offers assistance on a day-to-day basis in the broad program areas of economic development and employment, education, family and individual services, health, housing, and community resources.

The Urban League was Henry's first national civic engagement. He worked first on the Health and Welfare Committee and subsequently was asked to serve on the National Urban League Housing Program and was the first president of the National Urban League Foundation.

On September 6, 1959, Henry served on a panel for the National Urban League Conference along with the Citizens Planning and Housing Association, and the Greater Baltimore Committee—composed of the hundred biggest and most influential businessmen in the community. The title of the panel session was "Working with Changing Neighborhoods." Henry made a presentation entitled "Wholesale departure of whites as Negroes move in." He discussed with the group the effective use of citizen groups in establishing better neighborhoods for

Negroes. He identified the big issue in real estate sales was the problem of white realtors steering Negroes to communities that whites were fleeing.

Henry informed the group of an organization in the city called the Greater Baltimore Committee, which was composed of the hundred biggest and most influential businessmen in the community. This group was dedicated to the orderly growth of the community and spent most of its time in the past developing a program in the areas of physical planning. Henry stated, after many meetings and debates between the Greater Baltimore Committee, the Urban League, the Citizen's Planning and Housing Association, and influential neighborhood associations that Negro programs were accepted and added to the programs of the Greater Baltimore Committee, thus the Negro could enjoy improved communities with the help of neighborhood citizen groups.

Through Henry's association and membership with the Greater Baltimore Committee, he was able to bridge relationships between the Negro community and white business and neighborhood planners. Henry was a member of the National Urban League housing committee and maintained his real estate license, thus he was familiar with housing issues in minority communities and was the best person at the time to build these bridges.

In 1967, Henry was the speaker for the Forty-Ninth Annual Fellowship Dinner of the Westchester Urban League held at the Glen Island Casino. The theme of his speech was "The entrance of the Negro into the business and industrial world in an administrative capacity is a necessity if he is to become a full-fledged member of the American team." He stated that

> the Negroes are taught not to like themselves, not to be ambitious, to seek their rewards in heaven . . . We must free our minds from madness and strive for human rights and human dignity through industry. This is the solid rock on which we must build, and through which the Negro can maintain a substantial middle class group in this nation . . . I call upon the Negros to break out of the ghettoized thinking and get into the main stream of American life . . . So many of our great minds have gone into social work and education that should instead have gone into the business world. As things now stand, the money that Negros earn goes right back into [white] business and out of the Negro community.

In 1968, Henry gives a speech at the Urban League's National Conference on Social Welfare presented at the 1968 divisional program in San Francisco, California. Henry stated that there are only three alternatives to social welfare: the first is genocide, the model being set by Adolf Hitler; the second, apartheid, our model being Verwoerd's South Africa; and the third is the path of reason and responsibility, and this we can surely follow. It means closing the gap that separates our two nations, ending racism and giving Negroes an equal share in both the rewards and the responsibilities of citizenship. Our models here are the American constitution and the Judeo-Christian ethic. Only in this way can justice be served and democracy survive. "All that is necessary for the triumph of evil is that good men do nothing."

On November 19, 1968, Henry accepted the Urban League's Achievement Award. The award was presented at the Urban League Equal Opportunity Day dinner at the New York Hilton. The award was in recognition of notable success and for contributions to the goal of equal opportunity through a career that brilliantly exemplified the fulfillment of the American dream. He began his acceptance speech by saying, "By absolute dollar measure our business [H. G. Parks Inc.] activity is insignificant. It does become relatively important however when we view the earnings of our spot in the general market by direct application, without subsidy, of unique but sound business practices."

As a member of the National Urban League board of trustees, Henry was asked to give testimony before the small business subcommittee, the committee on banking and currency, and United States Senate on federal programs for minority enterprise on Thursday, December 11, 1969.

Henry began his testimony by defining minority enterprise as the sum total of efforts made to facilitate the entrance of minorities into business on a successful basis. He went on to describe the concept of black enterprise that took on a formal image in the 1900s when Booker T. Washington founded the National Business League without benefit of national support until President Richard Nixon, in his "Bridges to Human Dignity" speeches of 1968, called for a national program of black enterprise. The president followed up this campaign promise by issuing Executive Order 11458 on March 5, 1969. The executive order established the office of minority business enterprise, whose major functions were described in the federal register, volume 34, number 75.

Henry proceeded to give a fourteen-page chronology of federal legislation, closing his remarks with "Mr. Chairman, let me say that people in the disadvantaged communities of this country have no faith in federal programs for minority enterprise as they are currently administered. These programs have, no doubt, assisted many minority businessmen, but for every one helped, there are untold thousands who have met a negative response, and who have decided that the federal government is not sincere in its efforts."

Henry provided the requested testimony for the Urban League, but he said he hated to do it. Henry said it felt like begging, and begging was humiliating. Henry believed blacks did not need to beg anymore. He had demonstrated at H. G. Parks Inc. that blacks can compete on equal terms with anyone. He is quoted: "I think we need to learn how to be managers and how to operate profitable businesses, because we will never learn how to be strong as a people until we begin to have some self-sufficiency, to own, to have access to the money and the proper use of it."

Henry wrote to Vernon Jordan, resigning from the National Urban League effective February 15, 1972, having served thirty-seven continuous years. The Urban League honored Henry for his service on August 1, 1972.

Alpha Phi Alpha Fraternity, Kappa Chapter

While in college at Ohio State University, Henry became a member of the Alpha Phi Alpha Fraternity in 1936. Henry became a life member at a meeting in Chicago, Illinois, on December 30, 1952. In 1968, Henry was honored by the Alpha Phi Alpha Fraternity at the annual convention in Detroit, Michigan, for outstanding contributions to business. On March 1, 1982, he received the Alpha Phi Alpha thirty-year life membership shingle in recognition of his loyalty to and continued interest in the organization. In various settings, Henry was financially generous to the fraternity and affiliate chapters.

National Association for the Advancement of Colored People (NAACP)

W. E. B. Du Bois founded the National Association for the Advancement of Colored People in 1909. Henry had been a member since his early childhood and became a life member in 1955.

In 1981, the NAACP corporate support committee wrote to Henry seeking his support for one of their national corporate fund-raising campaigns. In 1980, 509 United States corporations contributed $2.1 million to the NAACP national fund-raiser, however 80 corporations among the top 250 Fortune companies did not contribute to the NAACP fund-raising campaign.

Since Henry was known and becoming well-established in corporate circles, he was contacted by the NAACP to indicate, where possible, how or through whom they might approach companies that were nonsupporter of the fund-raiser. The Signal Companies where Henry was on the board of directors was on the list as a noncontributor at the time. Henry wrote the Signal Companies immediately, seeking support, and they favorably responded.

In 1986, the Baltimore branch of the NAACP identified and contracted to purchase a building to serve as a permanent headquarters. Ms. Enolia P. McMillan, president, sought Henry's support for the $100,000 fund-raiser. Mr. Jake Oliver, publisher of the *Afro-American* newspapers, and Mr. Martin Resnick, owner of Martins Caters—both of Baltimore—served as co-chair for the fund-raiser. Henry was able to get support from most Baltimore corporations through his membership on the Greater Baltimore Committee. Most of the surrounding companies supported the NAACP because they knew of Henry's integrity and connections with the black community.

Goucher College

Henry was elected, in July 1969, to serve on the board of trustees of Goucher College in Towson, Maryland. Goucher College was, at the time, an independent liberal arts college for women and was founded in Baltimore in 1885. It is located on three hundred acres in Towson, Maryland. Henry was the first black to serve on their board. The black community was pleased with this appointment because it gave another option for black women to become well educated. Both women and men supported Henry's appointment to the college's board of trustees.

Provident Hospital

In 1970, Henry was appointed to the board of directors and board of trustees of Provident Hospital. Henry worked with the hospital's administration from 1969 to 1971. Henry served on the building committee for a new facility located on Liberty Heights Avenue. Prior to the new location, Provident Hospital was located in the black community at 1514 Division Street, Baltimore, Maryland. While on the board of directors, Henry served on the committee for studying and interpreting consultant management reports and the ad hoc committee on investments. While on the board of trustees, he served on the executive committee, budget and finance. Henry resigned on January 27, 1971, fatigued from working on too many boards that took significant time from H. G. Parks Inc.

The Johns Hopkins University Center
for Metropolitan Planning and Research

During 1981, Henry was invited to consult with the Johns Hopkins University Center for Metropolitan Planning and Research. After several meetings and through Henry's relationship with the Greater Baltimore Committee, the Greater Baltimore Committee's subcommittee report on minority business development was approved and strongly supported. The idea started through Henry's contact with one of the faculty members at the Johns Hopkins University Center for Metropolitan Planning and Research, Dr. Robert Hearn.

Arena Players Inc.

In 1981, Henry supported the Baltimore Arena Players in their fund-raising campaign. Henry used his influence to leverage dollars from major corporations regionally and nationally to support the Arena Players just as he had helped the NAACP with their fund-raising campaigns.

Davison Chemical Division, which locally represented the W. R. Grace & Company, contributed $75,000 to the Arena Players for the 1981 fund-raiser campaign. The check was presented by Henry, who was vice chair of the board of Arena Players Inc. The money was allocated to the capital improvement budget to transform a dilapidated building on Orchard Street to a three-story modern theater to include a modern dance studio, rehearsal rooms, classroom facilities, and the youth theater and set design/building areas.

In 1986, W. R. Grace & Company and Signal Companies contributed to the Arena Players two-for-one matching program. W. R. Grace & Company Inc. contributed $5,000, the Signal Companies Inc. contributed $1,000, and the Baltimore Chapter of Links Inc. contributed $1,000. The video recording of the annual giving event was aired November 10, 1986.

The National Dental Association

Henry received the 1983 Special Recognition Award for pioneer in business achievement at the seventieth annual convention of the National Dental Association civil rights scholarship fund-raising dinner. Founded in 1913, the tristate dental association of Maryland, Virginia, and the District of Columbia and the National Dental Association were celebrating seventy years of leadership, achievement, and commitment to excellence in dentistry at the convention. The association provided a national forum for black and minority dentists and has advocated quality health care for all citizens, particularly low-income and minority citizens.

The Interracial Council for Business Opportunity

The Interracial Council for Business Opportunity represented private sector support as the advocate for the free-enterprise system for minorities, helping them to start, expand, and acquire their own businesses. They provided management training programs, served as consultants to minority businesspersons, and assisted minority businesses to sell their products and services to private sector companies. The council was a prototype for minority economic development. The Ford Foundation was a significant contributor. The council was located in New York City.

Henry was very active with the council and was asked to be honorary chairperson for the twentieth anniversary annual dinner on April 27, 1983. Henry was a sponsor for the 1984 dinner held on April 25 at the New York Hilton. Henry was invited to serve in these highly visible roles because of his corporate name recognition and his known interest in the advancement of minorities in American business.

The United Negro College Fund

Henry was nominated to the board of directors of the United Negro College Fund on February 10, 1987. He had been affiliated with the group years prior and served as chair of the corporate committee in 1972. While serving as a member of the board of directors on the First Pennsylvania Corporation, First Pennsylvania contributed forty shares of stock to the United Negro College Fund fund-raiser. The gift was worth $2,080 more than any donor had given for the fund-raiser. The United Negro College Fund fund-raiser goal was $85,000, and with Henry's participation and leadership, it was reached.

In 1986, Warner-Lambert, where Henry was also on the board pledged one million dollars to the United Negro College Fund. RJR Nabisco Inc. also pledged one million dollars the same year.

Black Enterprise Magazine

In 1973, 1974, and 1975 issues of *Black Enterprise* magazine, H. G. Parks Inc. was ranked among the top ten of one hundred top black-controlled businesses in the United States.

Henry served on the board of advisers of *Black Enterprise* magazine and was instrumental in helping them accomplish their goals. Henry was proud of the contributions the magazine made to the black business community and others who read the publication, but he maintained his reservations about identifying H. G. Parks Inc. with *black*.

In a letter dated December 20, 1972, Henry wrote to publisher Mr. Earl G. Graves:

> It may seem strange to you but I really do not care to have our business listed as a black anything or categorized in a special sense so as to arouse "social concerns" at the table or at the point of purchase. Our business is consumer oriented and there is no value in "waving flags."
>
> Your cover letter refers to "black-owned businesses." Our controlling interest happens to be black but I assure you that we have

made every effort to see that our stock is generally distributed and that we have *properly* integrated our organization.

We have accomplished a number of things that black people have never done before but we look upon this as opening doors so that others may follow.

Maryland Magazine, published quarterly by the department of economic and community development, was preparing an article for a forthcoming issue using black-owned businesses across the state. Henry replied in a similar manner as he did with *Black Enterprise* magazine: "We would rather not be a part of the kind of story that you are planning. It does us absolutely no good to be 'pinpointed' in the market place in this manner. Our business, 'believe it or not', is the only business of its type operating in the general consumer market."

Henry tired of media sources referring to H. G. Parks Inc. as Negro or black. He sold his product to the general public, and he did not discriminate against anyone who wanted to enjoy his products. He simply wanted to be a *businessman.*

In a speech given on May 26, 1977, at the *Black Enterprise* 100 announcement luncheon held at the Civic Center in Atlanta, Georgia, Henry applauded *Black Enterprise* for its job of creating hero images in the black community that displaced the negative images that were more often portrayed.

CHAPTER 5

Honors and Recognitions

This is my first and last honorary degree.
— Henry G. Parks Jr.

The *New York Amsterdam News*

In 1954, the *New York Amsterdam News* awarded Henry a community business citation "for his devotion to the highest American business principles, helping to lay the foundation upon which to build the structure of the economic welfare of the Negro community, and for his initiative, foresight, and belief in the American ideal of free enterprise" (C. B. Powell, president and editor).

Young Men's Christian Association (YMCA)

Henry remained active in the Young Men's Christian Association since childhood. The YMCA of Baltimore, Druid Hill Avenue Branch, gave Henry awards for conspicuous service almost every year after his move to Baltimore. He was an annual financial supporter to this organization for decades.

The District of Columbia Chamber of Commerce

The District of Columbia Chamber of Commerce honored Henry at its small-business annual award dinner held at the presidential ballroom, Hotel Statler-Hilton, Washington, DC, on October 27, 1962. Henry was well-known in Washington, DC, for his products and engagement in community and civic engagement.

The *New York Courier*

The Philadelphia Cotillion Society honored Henry along with Roy Wilkins and Edward Brooke on January 3, 1963, at the Society's Fifteenth Annual Christmas Cotillion in the Grand Ballroom and Trianon Suite of the Hilton Rockefeller Center in New York. Henry was named for his aggressiveness and business acumen. His company provided employment for hundreds. His progressive advertising methods were met with national acclaim. Mr. Roy Wilkins was awarded for his sustained courage and fortitude in steering the National Association for the Advancement of Colored People (NAACP) through one of the most crucial and controversial periods of American Negro history. Mr. Brooke was honored for holding the highest elective office of any Negro in the United States and having an outstanding achievement record. Some of the sponsors for the event included Dr. Ralph J. Bunche, Jackie Robinson, Marian Anderson, Alfred Gwynne Vanderbilt, Joan Crawford, Arthur Spingarn, Pearl Buck, A. Philip Randolph, and others.

The Small Business Men's League of Baltimore

In 1963, Henry was selected Man of the Year by the Small Business Men's League of Baltimore.

Philadelphia Citizens Selection Committee

Henry received the Fifth Philadelphia Citizens Selection Committee Award of Merit on October 7, 1966, at a dinner at the Sheraton Hotel. This was the committee's highest award. He was cited for his "exemplification of the Negro man and his outstanding contribution to the civic and political life in America." The proceeds from the dinner benefitted the United Negro College Fund and the Association for Study of Negro Life and History. James H. J. Tate was mayor and William W. Scranton was governor.

The Greater New Haven
Business and Professional Men's Association

The Greater New Haven Business and Professional Men's Association Award was presented to Henry for exceptional contribution to the implementation of black economic and business development on a national basis on October 31, 1969.

The H. G. Parks Inc. Employees

Employees of H. G. Parks Inc. honored Henry at the twentieth-year anniversary of the company in May 1971. This honor was bestowed at the Twentieth Annual Sales Meeting held in Baltimore.

The dedication from the employees read,

> In the last twenty years, our company has written one of the greatest success stories in meat-marketing history.
>
> Henry G. Parks, Jr. deserves credit, in large part, as the author of our success story. His vision and determination have taken us from our beginning in a converted old dairy plant, to our present ultra-modern, multi-million dollar facility.
>
> His imagination and drive have taken us from Baltimore neighborhood sales to retail distribution in virtually every store chain and independent from the tip of Virginia, northward along the eastern seaboard through Massachusetts.
>
> Once, Parks famous flavored sausage and scrapple were unknown commodities. Now, as a result of his untiring efforts, national recognition has come to our company and its product.
>
> But Henry G. Parks, Jr., the founder and president of our company, is more than the author of a business success story to many of the Parks people.
>
> We see him as the hero of our adventure as well. He has remained our leader because he truly leads. He sets the standard for us to match.
>
> He provides the example that encourages us to do our work well and to search for better ways to do it.
>
> Because he has made it possible for us to share in this success, we dedicate this twentieth annual sales meeting of H. G. Parks, Inc. to Henry G. Parks, Jr.

The Baltimore Frontiers Club

In 1973, the Baltimore Frontiers Club awarded Henry the distinguished citation to the H. G. Parks Inc. in recognition of its corporate efforts to uplift the quality of urban life.

Temple University

Henry was conferred an honorary doctorate of law from Temple University, Philadelphia, Pennsylvania, on May 29, 1975. Marvin Wachman was president, and this was the Eighty-Ninth Annual Commencement Exercise. Arthur A. Koch, a member of the graduating class, introduced Henry for his degree presentation. David P. Eastburn, Robert J. McCloskey, Waldo Emerson Nelson, Max Rudolf, and Martha Peterson also received honorary degrees. Dr. Martha Peterson, president of Barnard College, was the commencement speaker—the third woman in Temple's history to speak at a commencement. Henry was quoted in the *Evening Bulletin*: "This is my first . . . and last honorary degree." He did not like the pageantry and ceremony at the civic center convention hall. A total of 6,200 students received degrees and six honorary awards. This all made Henry crazy. There were too many people for him.

He wrote to Marvin Wachman, president; Carol B. Boerer, office of special events; and Mr. and Mrs. Koch a few days afterward, thanking them for the honor and the arrangement made for him and his daughter to attend the exercises. Henry was a friend to Philadelphia, serving as director of the First Pennsylvania Corporation, dedicating himself to the principles of equal opportunity, human rights, and justice under the law. Henry was fifty-nine years of age, but little did he know that Morgan State University was making similar plans to recognize and honor him the following year.

On May 31, 1975, the *Pittsburgh Courier* wrote an article with the cover that read: "Black businessman gets degree." Henry still did not understand why he was referred to as a black businessman. He was a *businessman*.

Morgan State University

Although Henry stated that his honorary doctorate from Temple University in 1975 was his first and last, Morgan State University conferred a second honorary doctorate of humane letters on May 30, 1976. Enolia P. McMillan was chairman of the board of directors, and Andrew Billingsley was president. Henry was described as nationally known for founding and nurturing one of the most successful black-owned businesses in the United States and was cited as having a sterling life of service to the Baltimore community, serving in leadership roles of former city councilman, the Community Cablevision Systems of Maryland, the Opportunities Industrialization Center, Provident Hospital, the Baltimore Chapter of the American Red Cross, the National Urban League, the Community Chest of Baltimore, the Maryland Judiciary Selection Council, Baltimore Neighborhoods Inc., the United Negro College Fund, and Goucher College. Honorary degrees

were also conferred on Verda Freeman Welcome, Steven Muller, Howard Lee
Cornish, Elizabeth Murphy Moss, and Margaret Walker Alexander.

Junior Achievement of Metropolitan Baltimore

Junior Achievement of Metropolitan Baltimore inducted H. G. Parks Inc. into
the Business Hall of Fame in 1981. The purpose of the Business Hall of Fame was
created to provide Baltimore business leaders, past and present, recognition for
their significant contributions to the growth and development of business in the
community. The Greater Baltimore Committee helped to establish the Hall of
Fame and continues to research in the selection of laureates.

Founded in 1919, Junior Achievement is the world's oldest privately funded
economic and business education organization. The purpose is to provide
young people with practical economic education programs and experiences in
a competitive private enterprise system through partnership with business and
education communities. Junior Achievement offers a wide range of programs
targeted toward elementary, middle, and high school students. These programs
are designed to provide young people the tools necessary to become more-and
better-informed employees, employers, consumers, and leaders of the future.

Arena Players Inc.

The first Arena Players Special Award was presented to Henry. The award
was given by the players group. Its purpose was to express in a tangible way the
appreciation of the group to an individual whose contribution to the well-being of
the Arena Players organization had set an example for all. Henry was a longtime
patron of the Arena Players and served as member of the board of directors, vice
president, and chairman of the fund-raising committee since 1980. The award
was presented to Henry with gratitude in recognition of his vision, his wisdom, his
compassion, and his generosity in furthering the theatrical organization.

The Baltimore Marketing Association Inc.

The Baltimore Marketing Association inducted Henry in the Black Business
Hall of Fame on December 9, 1982, at the Fourteenth Annual Business Award
presentation; 1982 was the first year of the hall of fame. Eight individuals who,
because of their business achievements and contributions to the community,
shall reign in our minds as men and women of extraordinary faith and courage.
This recognition helps adults and youth understand the nature of the pride that

spirited them to overcome their circumstances and rise victoriously in their fight to uplift black people and to ensure that youth know the great black pioneers in business that have already laid the pathways for them. The event was held at the Baltimore Hilton Hotel.

The Baltimore Marketing Association Inc. was organized in October 1967 for the purposes of improving, through its membership, the marketing and public relations programs that many corporate organizations direct to minority consumer markets. The membership consists of persons and organizations within the fields of commerce, business, industry, and education. Through the John Sheppard Scholarship Fund, deserving minority students majoring in business or related fields are awarded financial assistance.

Other inductees included Nelson Wells, 1786-1843; Isaac Myers, 1835-1891; John H. Murphy Sr., 1840-1922; Josiah Diggs, 1864-1938; Charles Shipley, 1879-1943; Robert Coleman, 1877-1946; and Pauline B. Brooks, 1915-

Congressman Paul Sarbanes saluted Henry on the United States Senate floor for his accomplishments and contributions for his pioneering and path-breaking efforts that have enhanced the civic and commercial life of Baltimore.

The Greater Baltimore Committee

Greater Baltimore Committee selected Henry for the Jefferson Miller award for civic accomplishment on April 21, 1983. The award was established in 1969 to pay tribute to Mr. Miller in recognition of the tenth anniversary of his leadership in the redevelopment of downtown Baltimore by his dedicated efforts as general manager of the Charles Center project. Each year since then, an individual has been selected who has displayed outstanding civic accomplishment. Mayor Schaefer and Dr. Milton S. Eisenhower were past recipients of the award. The ceremony was held at the Hyatt Regency Baltimore. Richard P. Sullivan was chair of the Greater Baltimore Committee. The *Baltimore Sun Papers* reported on Sunday, April 24, 1983: "Parks lauded for citizenship by the Greater Baltimore Committee, annual citizenship award."

The United Negro College Fund Inc.

Henry and John G. Smale, chairman and chief executive of Procter & Gamble Company, received the 1987 Frederick D. Patterson Award in recognition of their support for black higher education. The award was presented on behalf of forty-three private, historically black colleges and their forty-five thousand students. Mrs. Nancy Reagan and Ms. Leontyne Price were previous recipients of the award. The United Negro College Fund hosted the forty-third anniversary

dinner at the Waldorf Astoria on March 12, 1987. The dinner chairman was John
H. Johnson, president and publisher of Johnson Publishing Company Inc. in
Chicago, Illinois.

Warner-Lambert Company

Warner-Lambert recommended Henry for the United Negro College Fund
Frederick D. Patterson Award. On April 27, 1987, Warner-Lambert hosted a
second dinner in Henry's honor to celebrate his ten years of service on the
Warner-Lambert board of directors. The event was held at the Hilton Parsippany,
New Jersey. Henry invited his two daughters, Grace Parks Johnson and Cheryl
Parks, his grandson Marc Johnson, Alice Pinderhughes, William Quinn, Luther
and Callie Johnson, and Cynthia Bond. Warner-Lambert presented Henry with a
sterling silver tray for his service as board member from 1977 to 1987 and made a
financial commitment to the United Negro College Fund.

Warner-Lambert additionally hosted a retirement dinner for Henry at the
Baltimore Center Club on June 23, 1987. Henry's health was failing at this point,
and he was anxious to reduce his scheduled activities.

Chapter 6

Family

Siblings

Daddy liked Jeanne and Mother liked Henry.
                                    —Vera Wilson

Henry had two sisters, Jeanne and Vera. He loved both of his sisters, and his sister Vera, in an interview, said, "Henry used to hold our hands when we walked down the street. He was our big brother."

Jeanne was her father's heart. The family knew Henry Sr. favored Jeanne and their mother favored Henry. Jeanne was extroverted, bold, and sassy. Jeanne knew that Henry was more of a mother's boy, but she did not care; he was her big brother, and she expected him to take care of and look out for her.

In school, Jeanne liked the boys, and the boys liked Jeanne. She would go out every night of the week, constantly, Vera would recall. She dated four and five boys at one time. There was no judgment in Vera's voice. This was just the fact.

Jeanne was as beautiful as Henry was handsome. She left home for New York City at age fifteen. She was too young. She was beautiful, and Henry described her as a fair singer. She was a vocalist who had her own band and club in Paris, France. Henry helped her finance the club. She socialized with Thurgood Marshall and Malcolm X. She and Thurgood Marshall were photographed together in *Sepia* magazine, July 1955. Henry would send Jeanne money every month, and if it did not arrive on time, she would call Henry and say, "Where is my money?" Henry knew she was living too fast, but being in another country, he had little control, but he worried about her. Jeanne died from a heroin addiction, and Henry was heartbroken.

I met and interviewed Vera at her home in Washington, DC. She and her husband, Clay, hosted a luncheon for Henry and me. Henry said Vera and Clay hosted numerous parties at their home. Henry brought all his friends to Vera and Clay's.

It was clear upon entry to their home that Vera loved Henry, and Henry loved Vera.

Vera was the youngest of the three children. She was high-spirited and inspirational. As a child, Vera had scarlet fever and a stroke that left her paralyzed and bedridden. Some years later, there was a house fire next door to the Parks's family house. Seeing the embers from a window flying in the air outside of the house, someone inside the Parks's home yelled, "The house is on fire!" Henry said that from a paralyzed state, Vera sat up in the bed and somehow got out of the bed and started to walk. This became a long-standing laughable moment for the family. Vera had always been referred to as the weaker child, but after physical therapy, Vera gained full mobility. She attended college and married Clay Wilson, who also worked at the Crayton's Southern Sausage Company Inc. where Henry and "Little Willie" had part ownership. Vera gave birth to Clay Wilson III. She was proud of her son.

At the dining table, Vera said, "Daddy liked Jeanne and Mother liked Henry." She was unperturbed about how her parents saw her. She was happy and enthusiastic. Henry especially loved Vera because he said she had every reason to be angry with God, but instead, she was the most positive person he had ever known. Henry always described Vera as the happiest and most content of the three Parks children. She never had the needs of Henry or Jeanne.

Vera married Clay Wilson, who, early in his career, worked at the Crayton's Sausage Plant in Dayton. When Clay and Vera moved to Washington, he worked at the White House in catering. The walls of their home were filled with photographs taken at the White House. This was a real sense of pride for Clay. When Henry and I visited Clay and Vera's house, Clay took a real affection toward me that Henry noticed. As we drove back to Baltimore, Henry said, "Clay really liked you!"

When Henry learned that Clay had died, he was deeply upset about the death and very concerned about Vera. I drove Henry everywhere he and I traveled together, so it was natural for him to ask me to drive to Washington to see his sister. On the day that he asked, I could not drive. It was the only time Henry was deflated with me. He said to me, "If I have to crawl to see my sister, I will." He recovered and we continued.

Marriage

I married whom I wanted to marry.
—Henry G. Parks Jr.

On August 9, 1938, Henry married Virginia Byrd, daughter of Mr. and Mrs. James Byrd of Wilberforce. They met at Wilberforce University where Henry was director of the National Youth Administration Project. Virginia Byrd was born in Columbus, Ohio, and attended local schools. She was a home economics major and graduated from Wilberforce University. She worked at Florida A&M University in the late 1930s before moving to Indianapolis, Indiana, where she taught at Crispus Attucks High School. She was a member of the Alpha Kappa Alpha Sorority.

Although I had the pleasure of meeting the former Mrs. Parks, I never interviewed her for this book. Henry felt that the marriage was off to a bad start because she came to the marriage with debts, and being the money manager he was, he did not like that. Henry said he ended up paying for the whole wedding, and he didn't like this. Henry thought the bride's parents should have sponsored the wedding as was tradition.

Henry stated that there were a number of problems from the start. One incident in the marriage that appeared to bother him most was Mrs. Parks's jealousy over Henry's love of roses. Henry had cultivated from his mother a love for roses. Mrs. Parks thought Henry placed more attachment on roses than to her and the children. Henry said she decided to have slipcovers made in a rose-patterned fabric and have the living room walls papered in a pattern of red roses. When Henry saw what she had done, he asked her why she had done such a thing. She replied, "Well, you like roses so much." He was livid. Henry was still livid during our interview and said, "Idiot!"

Mrs. Parks was often frustrated in the marriage because she wanted to socialize, and Henry wanted to find his niche in the business world. Henry worked long hours and was never home. As a consequence, she believed every problem within the marriage and household was his.

Mrs. Parks reported to Henry when he returned home from work that the black children at school were throwing stones at their daughters. Henry asked his wife, "Why would they do something like that?" Mrs. Parks replied, "Because they thought the girls were white." Henry's daughters were beautiful and very fair of complexion, as was Mrs. Parks. While telling me this story, Henry got tears in his eyes and said, "Can you believe that? Someone would try to hurt my children." Henry told the story with such pain. It was as if the stones were being thrown directly at him and me as well. Listening, I was saddened but knew children can be cruel.

Unlike men who are indiscreet with women, Henry humorously acknowledged his indiscretions with men. From my determination, he didn't appear to think anything was wrong with it. His logical thinking was familiar to me—chauvinistic. He thought like other men I knew: if the wife was well provided for, then men had a license to do whatever they wanted, usually discreetly.

In 1953, after approximately fifteen years of marriage, Mrs. Parks wanted a divorce. Henry did not understand why nor did he want a divorce. He said he thought he was a good provider, she had a good allowance, and she had a car. He said, "What black woman had that?"

A year after the divorce, Mrs. Parks married James Hilliard, who, Henry said, was a military officer. Henry was not happy about this at all; it was like a slap in the face, and he wondered how long that relationship had been going on. In addition to, who was this man who was going to be around his daughters? He was hot and, I suspect, unforgiving.

Henry paid for the divorce Virginia requested. He paid child support and traveled to New York to visit his daughters. Virginia initially refused to move to Baltimore.

She divorced Mr. Hilliard in 1957, and in 1989, she married Daniel Weatherford, who died in 1993.

When Mrs. Parks moved to Baltimore, she taught home economics at Pimlico, Roland Park, and Green Spring Junior High Schools.

Years later, when the Parks Sausage Company became successful, the former Mrs. Parks claimed Henry's success was due to her recipe. When I asked Henry if this was true, he emphatically said, "*No!* The Parks Sausage recipe I developed myself using certain cuts of meat and spices from around the world. She used my sausage in her recipes."

Still on the interview on love and marriage, I finally asked, "Who was the love of your life?" Henry replied with the name of a married man who had died years earlier. Henry said, "I was not sure I was going to make it when he died," then he followed saying, "but I married who I wanted to marry." *What? What a conundrum*, I thought. There was duality in Henry during his marriage. Regardless of his personal rationale, at this point in history, Henry had to be married. It was out of the question, and especially in American business, not to be married. However, in defense of Mrs. Parks, I thought every man or woman discerns when their spouse's *heart* is somewhere else. Through it all, when I visited Henry's home or office, he maintained photographs of his wife and children. He was honest and loving in his conversations about his wife and children. He never remarried. This was his family.

Children and Grandchildren

I love my children.

—Henry G. Parks Jr.

In my conversations with Henry, he would say, "I love my children," and "I have taken care of my children."

Five years in Henry and Virginia's marriage, Grace Gaynell was born in 1943. I thought Grace was a delightful and funny person with a strong mind and serious like Henry at times. Grace married Sinclair Johnson and gave birth to three very handsome children: Marc Henry Johnson, Rosalie Virginia Johnson, and Dax Parks Johnson. Henry was stressed completely when Sinclair and Grace divorced.

After the divorce was final, Henry hoped that she would marry again to have some help with raising the children. I made many favorable comments about Grace. He considered me as an eligible candidate and took my compliments about his daughter as more. Looking over his eyeglasses, he asked, "Do you want to marry my daughter?"

In 1946, Cheryl Parks was born. Cheryl was a pleasant young lady and pretty too. She never married nor had children. Cheryl worked for Eastern Airlines as a stewardess and subsequently earned a college degree from Notre Dame of Baltimore.

Henry would often say he loved his children but that he really did not know them.

CHAPTER 7

Finale

Honored Wounds

No one escapes the world without some troubles and woes. If we are lucky, we find some peace along the way. Henry was not a man to trust very many people and did not publicly share his troubles. He was a man of his word when he frequently said, "Nothing is accomplished by being negative." However, he experienced tremendous pain and sorrow and some good times too.

Henry was born during a sad period of American racial history; however, many Negro men and women of the era were making advances on an uneven playing field in inventions, science, abolitionism, performing arts, music, sports, business, law, journalism, government, and politics.

Henry was born and died in an era between many notable African Americans: Thurgood Marshall, born July 2, 1908; Cab Calloway, born December 25, 1907; William "Count" Basie, born August 21, 1904; Dizzy Gillespie, born October 21, 1917; Lena Horne, born June 30, 1917; Ella Fitzgerald, born April 25, 1917; Pearl Bailey, born March 29, 1918; John H. Johnson, born January 19, 1918; Edward Brooke, born October 26, 1919; Nat King Cole, born March 17, 1919; Sugar Ray Robinson, born May 3, 1921; Shirley Chisholm, born November 30, 1924; Sammy Davis Jr. born December 8, 1925; Josephine Baker born June 3, 1906; and Malcolm X born May 19, 1925. All lived during this period. Henry always said to me that it is not the color of a person but the class of the person that made them successful.

Henry never had the relationship with his father in childhood that he would like to have had, giving away feelings of not being loved by his father. His father gave harsh punishments and never included Henry in his male activities of hunting and fishing because of his relationship with his mother. Must we, as boys, be required to choose one parent over the other?

Although he felt love from his mother and had wonderful experiences with her gardening, swimming, and playing tennis, Henry lived to see her deteriorate and die from Parkinson's disease. He provided the very best care for her, and his sister Vera said that Henry moved his mother from Dayton, Ohio, so that she could be cared for at the Johns Hopkins Hospital. This was a difficult time.

His sister Jeanne, whom he loved dearly, was as hard as nails, he said. Jeanne was beautiful and wild. Jeanne died from an addiction to heroin. Henry used to hold her hand as a child and was proud to be her "big brother." Henry always felt responsible for her death and felt he could have and should have done more. This was a guilt I did not think he needed to carry.

His marriage to Virginia had failed. In later years, his former wife, after two additional marriages, suggested to Henry that they get back together. I asked Henry why he did not accept the offer, but he replied, "Too much has happened in between." I believe he loved Virginia Byrd but could never overcome her blaming him for what he described as "everything." He said she brought debt to their marriage, that he paid for the wedding, that she wanted the divorce he didn't want; he paid for the divorce, and a year later, she was married to James Hilliard—a marriage he thought suspicious. Henry felt she faulted him. And I think he blamed her for not sticking with him while he was struggling to build H. G. Parks Inc.

The newspapers said that the former Mrs. Parks was at Henry's side when he died. Love and marriage always maintain mysterious and enduring connections even when the marriage fails. It goes beyond having children together.

His sister Vera, who was viewed as the weakest of the three Parks siblings because she had scarlet fever and a stroke that left her paralyzed in her right arm, outlived both him and Jeanne. Henry was deeply saddened by her paralysis.

Henry reflected on his years with the Crayton's Sausage Company and finally understood why the owner, Leroy Crayton, never wanted to expand his company as Henry's youthful energy wanted. In later years, when Henry was burned out from his ambition, he learned that it made good sense to manage a smaller company and not to spread oneself too thin as a better route. Working his business, serving on too many corporate boards, and serving in the local, state, and federal sectors was too much for him over a long period of time. Henry would always advise me, "Pace yourself."

By having William Adams as a silent partner, Henry never received the full benefit of his labors at H. G. Parks Inc. because a percent of all profits went to his silent partner, who did not work in the business. However, the company would not have existed without the financing Mr. Adams provided. Banks were not lending money to Negro businesses. This was the agreement resulting from discriminating people.

Henry took pride in saying, "I always took care of my children." He purchased homes, cars, and educated his grandchildren in private schools.

Henry's diagnosis of Parkinson's disease was a hard pill, and he suffered for years. His doctor was Albert Steiner, chief of surgery at Maryland General Hospital. Dr. Steiner was described by his son as a social liberal and was one of the first

Baltimore physicians to integrate his waiting room in the 1950s. His son described his father's office as a hodgepodge of ethnicity—the wealthy and the welfare moms, doctors, lawyers, and sanitation workers. He never charged cops or firemen or men of the cloth, hookers, transvestites, and a lot of old people. Henry thought he was a good man.

At the end of his honored wounds, Henry proved that an African American businessman can compete in the American economic system on the same terms as anyone else.

Healing Moments

With a thirty-year difference in our ages, many people wondered why Henry and I were so close. I was not the love of his life nor his wife, but we became friends at a time of need for both of us. At this point in his life, he was without companionship, and I had a very low self-esteem that he built up. In some ways, I think he longed for the kind of love he received from his mother and grandmother as a child. Of course, I could not provide that, but I was a friend. We had no strings. I accepted Henry unconditionally, and he accepted me unconditionally. I had his private telephone number at his office, and my calls were always received or returned immediately. His secretary was always a delight and was fully aware as to who was calling. I was always cheerful when he called me. We enjoyed face-to-face company as often as possible.

The most important connection for me was that I saw my life somewhere in Henry's life. We both had fathers who loved us deeply but held lower ambitions for us than we held for ourselves, causing conflict and wounds in our self-esteem and the family. We were perceived as mother's boys. We each had the experience of being the only black in our classes in high school. We both experienced all the segregation, racism, oppression, and humiliation of high school and college life. At the same time, it was necessary for us to maintain a positive attitude when what we really felt was anger. Neither Henry nor I would give way to hatred. This takes a lot of energy for every black person who can do it. With all this, we were expected to move ahead too. We both experienced academic advisers who told us we did not belong and that essentially would never make it. We both learned that when your parents support you the best they can, you support yourself the best you can, and you are met head-on with deliberate road blocks. It is a tough lot.

On the other hand, Henry and I also had benevolent whites who helped us accomplish our dreams, and that was our alliance with the white community. Blacks who allied with whites are viewed as crossovers. The perception is that you are too white to be black and too black to be white. So where is the comfortable fit? And there were those who saw Henry as not militant enough toward issues of civil rights. I knew this feeling too.

At various times, Henry said the most endearing things to me, such as, "You know, Maurice, if I had a son, I would want him to be just like you." I never knew a person on earth who wanted a gay son. Henry made me *feel valued*.

When my partner and I built our home in Catonsville, I took Henry to see the house under construction. I described to Henry where the electrical sockets were being installed, plumbing fittings for the bathrooms and kitchen, floor and wall types, the lot topography, and window types. Henry looked and listened then said, "Maurice, if you can do this, man, you can do anything!" What I heard was his being totally *proud of me*. No one expressed being proud of me before.

Henry often referred to me as *bright*, a word I have never heard used to describe me.

Henry took me to the Center Club, one of Baltimore's most exclusive private clubs, located atop One Charles Center where he was a member. While dining with Henry, other members of the club would wave and say, "Hello, Mr. Parks." Sometimes, Henry would excuse himself from the table, and other times, they would briefly chat and exit. He seemed to be known by so many corporate people. I was so proud to be associated with him, and I had never seen the city as beautiful as it was from that very high elevation at night. He said, "Maurice, you are just about the only person I bring here frequently." With all the attention Henry received, he appeared sad, but on the other hand, there was something romantic about joining him there. He wanted to dine with me, and I wanted to be in his presence every chance I got. I have never had the experience of someone of Henry's stature ever wanting to spend time with me.

When Henry's company was planning to get him a new car, he asked me what type of car he should get. I was shocked that he would ask my opinion, and he asked me all the time on many of his decisions. He asked the same type of question when he sold his business. He said, "Maurice, what do you think I should do?" I was always amazed that he considered my opinion—an opinion I thought insignificant in that I felt there was a thirty-year deficit in my knowledge and experience compared to his.

When we first met in the mid-1970s, he asked my opinion so much I asked him to give me a job in his plant. I worked for the public school system and was paid from an annually renewed grant, similar to the one Henry worked on while working for Dr. Bethune. I never knew if I was going to get paid. He said, "Maurice, goddamn it, you would come down here and take over the business!" I laughed out loud. I really never understood the lens through which Henry saw me. But I knew it was a thousand times better than I saw myself.

Henry had a way of making me feel special. *Henry built me up!*

In return, I built him up too!

The very first time Henry informed me he was taking me to the Center Club, he said, "I am taking you to dinner. You need to wear a jacket and tie." Stress filled me at two levels: one, to be invited to the unknown, but more importantly, I could not afford the Brooks Brothers attire that Henry fashioned.

I squeezed money on a credit card and walked into Joseph Bank's. The sales representative got me suited in a navy blue blazer, white shirt, red-striped tie, and taupe slacks. On the evening of the dinner, I was filled with anxiety, wondering how this outfit was going to go over with Henry. He was not critical, but he could give a disapproving look. When I arrived at his home to pick him up, Henry looked at me and said, "Maurice that is as stylish as I have ever seen you." I glowed with relief. This meant he was pleased, and I was presentable. He had no idea what my soul had gone through to meet his approval.

I was always available and present when he called me. I stopped what I was doing and gave him my undivided attention. Sometimes he would call me at my job in Baltimore or Washington, DC, and say, "I want to see you tonight." I was always happy to see Henry, and moreover, I thought of all the people he had to select from, he chose me. I willingly drove us everywhere we traveled, in his car or mine. He would get frustrated with me if I was driving to a destination he was very familiar with because he wanted me to drive his way, which he thought was the absolute and most efficient way. He made me nervous but would laugh when I reflected on it. I thought, *To be that precise. What?*

He introduced me to his friends and family, and I introduced him to mine. Occasionally, I would pick him up at the Baltimore train station when he returned from his New York board meetings. Sometimes he would greet me with a smile, and other times he would be grumpy but would soon recover. He would apologize and say, "I don't mean to take this out on you." Few people ever apologized to me for their behavior. I was awed that he did. I was a commuter to and from Baltimore and Washington, DC. I completely understood his mood change.

Once I got tickets to the Kennedy Center for the Performing Arts in Washington, DC. I asked Henry and his dear friend Alice if they wanted to go, and he said yes. He and Alice sat in the back seat of his Cadillac as I drove to the performance. I had never had anyone entrust to me such an expensive car. I drove the Cadillac fast and hard to get there on time, but neither he nor Alice said a word. We had fun!

I could never afford to reciprocate the kinds of invitations that Henry offered me. Sometimes when he had an exhaustive day, I would purchase two thick steaks (he loved beef), baking potatoes, fresh lettuce, and garden tomatoes. When I arrived at his home, I would pour us a scotch and water. While I prepared the meal, we watched the local news. We would enjoy dinner, watching the world news. He would really enjoy being at home and would always say, "You can cook in my kitchen anytime!" Doing something nice for him made me happy.

Occasionally, on a Friday night, we would have a second scotch, and he would offer me a cigar. I thought they were horrible, but I would light up anyway. He never seemed to care if I wasted an extremely expensive cigar. I think he just wanted a companion. He was happy to have company in his home. He deserved it.

When Henry was diagnosed with Parkinson's disease, he described how he was putting things in order. He said he needed fifteen more years to complete his dream. I could not imagine from my lens what more he could have done. I was too young to really know the scope and depth of Parkinson's disease. It really saddened me to see his walking reduced to a shuffle.

When I was editor for the Alpha Phi Alpha Fraternity Delta Lambda Chapter newsletter, I wrote a cover story on Henry for the "Black History Month" issue. Although it was nothing compared to the attention he received from corporate America, he got a charge out of my featuring him—not because he needed more publicity, I think it was more that I had taken the time to do it. I drove him to the February monthly meeting with me, and he contributed five hundred dollars on the spot. The chapter needed the money. They were happy that he gave it, and I got points for bringing him to the chapter house. The brothers knew and honored us very quietly.

However these events get translated, we healed each other in unusual ways. At some moments, we were one.

Service of Memory

We thank you, God that although he walked with kings,
he never lost the common touch.
—Rev. Vernon N. Dobson

When Henry's daughter Grace informed me that Henry had died, I attended the viewing at Douglas Memorial Community Church before the official time so that I could have closure with this part of Henry's life. In my head, I could not reflect but just be.

Soon there were quiet moments with organ music.

I read the program: "We make no demands upon The Spirit: we ask nothing; we are in Thy presence as we are. O love of God, Love of God, do with us in this waiting moment what Thou wouldst do with us. We trust Thee, our God, as best we can, and beyond that we yield to Thy grace. Amen."

My mind slipped, and I recalled when I had visited Henry last at the nursing home. He was very sick and tired from the years of living with Parkinson's disease. He asked me to "please" disconnect him from tubes and cords. I knew exactly what he wanted. I whispered in his ear, "I love you but I can't do that." Then my heart just sank, and I cried.

I continued to read the program: GOD OF OUR LIFE, THROUGH ALL THE CIRCLING YEARS.

> God of our life, through all the circling years,
> We trust in Thee;
> In all the past, through all our hopes and fears,
> Thy hand we see.
> With each new day, when morning lifts the veil,
> We own Thy mercies, Lord, which never fail.
> God of the past, out times are in Thy hand;
> With us abide.
> Lead us by faith to hope's true promised land;
> Be Thou our Guide.
> With Thee to bless, the darkness shines as light,
> And faith's fair vision changes into sight.
> God of the coming years, through paths unknown
> We follow Thee;
> When we are strong, Lord leave us not alone;
> Our refuge be.
> Be Thou for us in life our daily bread,
> Our heart's true home when all our years
> Have sped. (Hugh T. Kerr)

I was glad Henry was no longer sick. I thought Henry's grandmother, who had taught him the Bible at an early age, was listening and was proud.

Alpha Phi Alpha Delta Fraternity brothers asked that I give a tribute to our fraternity brother on behalf of the Delta Lambda Chapter. I focused my tribute on several things that Henry and I had discussed in our conversations: He admired people who could do things that he could not do; he said he could easily assess where a person was and help them from that point; he would give them a chance; he believed in remaining positive; he believed you never get anywhere being negative; he never discriminated against social class or social differences; he thought time and money should be used wisely; and he believed in education and training. After my tribute, the Alpha brothers sang the Alpha Phi Alpha hymn.

I rode with Henry's daughters in the limousine to the Arbutus Memorial Park for entombment services and the receiving of friends.

Hours later, H. G. Parks Inc. officials and invited guests were gathered for the groundbreaking of the company's new $13 million home in the Park Circle Industrial Park enterprise zone.

Obituaries over the following days were in many leading national and local newspapers along the East Coast and as far west as California.

The *Baltimore Afro-American,* April 29, 1989, read: "800 attend rites for H. G. Parks, 72. United States Senator Paul Sarbanes, Governor William Donald Schaefer, Mayor Kurt L. Schmoke, former mayors Clarence Du Burns, and Thomas D'Alesandro, III attended the service. His lifelong friend and business associate, Samuel T. Daniels saw him as 'an unusually quiet architect of change, with tremendous concern for people and a necessity of providing equality of consideration for all.'"

JET magazine, May 15, 1989, Census: "Parks Sausage Co. Founder Henry G. Parks, 72 dies." *JET* described Henry as one of the nation's leading businessmen and a staunch civil rights advocate. In his role as Baltimore City Councilman, he pressed for laws opening public accommodations to blacks and easing bail requirements.

Black Enterprise magazine, June 1989, quoted Henry: "We need . . . to develop a class of black merchants. Let's start with the gas stations, the taverns, the services, the franchise's, and then go on to develop a larger entrepreneurships and move into corporate and other managerial posts . . . Let's locate our bright, yet untrained, young and give them training and guidance in business management. Let's locate the underemployed and motivate them. Let's encourage our young people to enroll in business colleges and seek MBAs. Let's, preach, and program for business development through our religious, fraternal and professional organizations and other message carriers."

The *Baltimore Sun Papers* wrote: "Mr. Parks' success was particularly impressive because he was a black man operating in a virtually all-white business world . . . Governor William Donald Schaefer, who served with Mr. Parks on the City Council during the 1960's and later appointed him to head the City Board of Fire Commissioner, called him yesterday 'A strong, wonderful man who stood up and fought on civil rights'" (April 25, 1989).

The obituary from public affairs commentator James Fleming, Henry Parks's model of a man, I thought was the best of all the obituaries I read. Fleming wrote,

> Henry G. Parks, Jr. may his tribe increase! In contemporary times, and in the Baltimore area, few if any individuals, have been more of what a man can become; few knew how he can rise above circumstances; how he can meet and overcome obstacles; How he can venture into untried waters; how he can challenge 'the system' without seeking to destroy it; and how he can bear frustrations in business and racial discrimination without hatefulness. In the end, his life was a success.
>
> Everything he touched did not turn into gold but he never became discouraged or bitter enough not to try and try again.
>
> He changed jobs often enough but he never stopped trying to find the niche which would be the fulfillment of his abilities, ambitions and training.

He was born in the deep south with no "silver spoon" and was raised in the segregated north, but was fortunate to have around him family and friends who, while they lived in battered neighborhoods, never allowed him to feel he was personally handicapped or that poverty was a life sentences . . . He regarded no failure as permanent or of having no value.

Neither did he consider any human "contact" uninteresting . . . That meeting with Adams remained a substantial friendship and partnership to the end of his days. Not only did Henry Parks build one of the larger meat processing operation in the country—the largest black-owned—but he loaned his influence, his training and his leadership to many sectors of civic and business life.

It is not surprising that he was a constant fundraiser for the United Negro College Fund, the NAACP and other civil rights groups, and that he was an early spiritual, as well as material, sponsor of such a useful local organization as Woman Power, Inc.

More surprising, perhaps, is that he also took time to serve a stint as a member of the Baltimore City Council. He added strength to the efforts to widen the bases of civil rights in the city and state and supported all people-enhancement programs. He also served seven years as president of the Board of Fire Commissioners and was often mentioned seriously for even high offices.

Henry Parks had a way of putting first things first. That is why he pursued the best higher education possible and never stopped studying.

He worked to build a strong food production business and surrounded himself with and energetic, resourceful ban of assistants; he wanted his enterprise to grow—to be an example of black achievement—and, therefore, never personally splurged in conspicuous consumption.

He also believed in the rightness of whites and African-Americans getting along together in mutual respect and helpfulness, and worked always to that end.

With this tapestry of his life, it was most fitting that groundbreaking for the new, multi-million-dollar Parks Sausage Company should take place last week April 24 on the very day that Henry Parks died.

With all that Henry accomplished in life personally and professionally, he lived simply. He liked a good hand of poker; he quit playing after a number of years because, as he said, "I am too lucky." He enjoyed a game of bridge; he said, "I am a good bridge player." He enjoyed swimming and tennis in his younger years. He owned a small collection of Haitian art. He enjoyed his solo travel to Haiti and Puerto Rico, his men's groups, a day at the races with the Swags, and from childhood to death, he enjoyed reading. The walls at his home on Reservoir Street were book lined. The former Mrs. Parks sent him books often. He stacked them on the floor by the director's chair that I sold to him years earlier.

Henry was very thoughtful at Christmastime. Each year, he would send the wives of his friends flowers; to the men he sent executive diaries with the Parks trademark on the back at the bottom, with personalization on the front; and Fin 'n Feather hams to family and closest friends. I was honored to be on this list.

I reflected on a Christmas when Henry and I were opening gifts. Henry laughed to himself, and he said to me as he opened a gift, "Guess what the mayor sent me for Christmas?"

I said, "What?"

Henry said, "Cookies. Can you imagine the mayor sending me *his* cookies?" And we laughed together.

Of all the people Henry knew and helped along the way, William Donald Schaefer, former mayor of Baltimore City and former governor of the state of Maryland, was the one who stood out to me as his best friend throughout the years.

Henry has left the earth, but he is still remembered. Civil rights embodied all he did. Through all his works, he wanted the public to know that all businesspeople are looking toward the sales they close with a reasonable profit, not the ones lost. Henry did not want to be recognized as a *Negro businessman* but a *businessman who was Negro*. Henry spent his career, in his private and public life, attempting to enlighten the world of the difference between the two. Almost one hundred years later, he is still defined by race *first*.

EPILOGUE

Six years after Henry's death, the *Washington Post* business section, July 15, 1995, wrote, "Parks Sausage Co. Ask MD for Help, Baltimore Firm Says $8 Million Needed to Stay in Operation." A food analyst from Ferris, Baker Watts Inc. in Baltimore stated that many of the company's wounds were self-inflicted. When the company moved its plant in 1990 to help make room for Oriole Park in Camden Yards, it built an expensive 133,000-square-foot factory that the company had hoped the company would grow into. But shortly after the move, Pizza Hut and Domino's Pizza switched to a lower-priced sausage supplier, which cost the company about 28 percent of its business.

The *Washington Post*, July 20, 1995: "A Sausage Maker's Md. Safety Net: More Parks Capital, Please." Parks is still a viable company recently ranking eighty-fifth on *Black Enterprise* magazine's list of the country's top one hundred black-owned service and industrial firms and eight among those in Maryland.

Washington Business, August 14, 1995: "Parks Sausage Gets a Reprieve." The company is giving a $400,000 line of credit from the Baltimore Development Corporation, allowing the company to remain open as it looks for an investor or buyer.

Alice Pinderhughes continued to invite me to many of her social functions. Some of her friends teased me because I always purchased corsages for her. The men collectively called me to the men's room and instructed me to stop giving Alice corsages because it was making them look bad in front of their wives. On one occasion, I was approached and encouraged to marry Alice after Henry's death because some of the old guard wanted to support her for mayor. When I drove Alice home after these events, we would laugh.

She called me to see if I had received money from Henry's estate. She said she had received hers and was elated. Henry's death affected us both deeply. She died of cancer on November 16, 1995. She was seventy-four. I was sad.

The *Washington Post*, May 26, 1996, wrote: "Parks Sausage Co. Closes, Laying off Its 219 Workers."

The *Washington Post*, Business, June 22, 1996, wrote: "Former Football Star to Buy Parks Sausage Co." Franco Harris, a former Pittsburgh Steelers running back turned snack-food entrepreneur, said he sees some daunting challenges ahead in turning around the company. "It feels fantastic, but I know that there's a lot of hard work ahead of us . . . I feel both very excited and very scared." The Harris deal seems to mark the end of a chapter in a long-running local business drama.

Henry's former wife Virginia Byrd-Parks-Hilliard-Weatherford died December 1999 from pneumonia at the age of eight-one. She lived in Baltimore.

Dr. Albert Steiner, otolaryngology chief surgeon at Maryland General Hospital, died in July 2000. In his obituary, his son Marc stated, "When one of his patients, Henry Parks of Parks Sausage, was there for surgery, Dad put him in a private room. The nurses had tried to put him in the colored ward, and Dad literally stood in the doorway and refused to let them move him. They had successfully integrated the hospital, which then began to dismantle the colored ward. He didn't abide any injustice and felt there should be no color line in America." Dr. Steiner was eighty-nine.

William Donald Schaefer, a political showman, former mayor of Baltimore City, and former governor of the state of Maryland and comptroller, died in April 2011. He was loyal to Henry all the way. He was eighty-nine.

Willie Adams, who went from being a numbers runner in the streets of Baltimore to the city's first prominent African American venture capitalist, died in June 2011 at the age of ninety-seven.

I have now fulfilled my promise to Henry to get this book completed. In a 2013 dream, Henry stood before a podium and said, "Maurice, I love you."

Appendix I

Deed of Gifts Donated to Baltimore City Life Museum by Maurice W. Dorsey August 22, 1989

DOCUMENTARY ARTIFACT, photograph, Fiftieth Anniversary Celebration Alpha Phi Alpha Fraternity Inc. August 7-11, 1956, Buffalo, New York, B/W

DOCUMENTARY ARTIFACT, photograph, B/W print, of awards dinner, Panoramic group, Philadelphia

DOCUMENTARY ARTIFACT, photograph, Henry Parks Jr. as a baby

DOCUMENTARY ARTIFACT, photograph, Henry Parks Jr.

DOCUMENTARY ARTIFACT, photograph, Woman linking sausages at Parks Sausage Meat Plant

DOCUMENTARY ARTIFACT, photograph, Man emptying pail into vat at Parks Sausage Meat Plant

DOCUMENTARY ARTIFACT, photograph, Woman w/dipper behind bags, Parks Sausage Meat Plant

DOCUMENTARY ARTIFACT, photograph, Close-up of hands and sausage, Parks Sausage Meat Plant

DOCUMENTARY ARTIFACT, photograph, Man packing sausage into box, Parks Sausage Meat Plant

DOCUMENTARY ARTIFACT, photograph, Overhead view of factory operations, Parks Sausage Meat Plant

DOCUMENTARY ARTIFACT, photograph, Man dumping large pail on gantry into press, Parks Sausage Meat Plant

DOCUMENTARY ARTIFACT, photograph, Man moving meat w/ tined fork, Parks Sausage Meat Plant

DOCUMENTARY ARTIFACT, photograph, Man using ladle in vat at Parks Sausage Meat Plant

DOCUMENTARY ARTIFACT, photograph, Man watching monitors, Parks Sausage Meat Plant

DOCUMENTARY ARTIFACT, photograph, Man looking from behind boxes, Parks Sausage Meat Plant

DOCUMENTARY ARTIFACT, photograph, Man checking the temperatures of sausage, Parks Sausage Meat Plant

DOCUMENTARY ARTIFACT, photograph, Assembly line of sausage packers, Parks Sausage Plant

DOCUMENTARY ARTIFACT, photograph, Man pushing meat into grinder, Parks Sausage Plant

DOCUMENTARY ARTIFACT, label, self-sticking w/ backing for Parks Rope Sausage, 16 oz., has blue band underneath the words 'Rope Sausage'

DOCUMENTARY ARTIFACT, label, self-sticking w/ backing for Parks Rope Sausage, 16 oz.

DOCUMENTARY ARTIFACT, label, self-sticking, w/ backing for Parks Hot Rope Sausage, 16 oz.

CONTAINER, Box, Packing, Flattened multicolored packing box for Parks Sausage, 12 oz. Hot n' Sagey Pork Sausage Patties

CONTAINER, Box, Packing, Flattened multicolored packing box for Parks Sausage, 10 oz. Hot n' Sagey Pork Sausage Patties

CONTAINER, Box, Packing, Flattened multicolored packing box for Parks Sausage, 6 oz. Brown n' Serve 8 Beef Sausage Links

CONTAINER, Box, Packing, Flattened multicolored packing box for Parks Sausage, 8 oz. Hot n' Sagey Sausage Brown n' Serve

CONTAINER, Box, Packing, Flattened multicolored packing box for Parks Sausage, 6 oz. Beef Sausage Links Brown n' Serve

CONTAINER, Box, Packing, Flattened multicolored packing box for Parks Sausage, 10 oz. 6 Natural Spice Sausage Patties

CONTAINER, Box, Packing, Flattened multicolored packing box for Parks Sausage, 12 oz. 6 Natural Spice Sausage Patties

CONTAINER, Box, Packing, Flattened multicolored packing box for Parks Sausage, 8 oz. 8 Pork n' Bacon Patties

CONTAINER, Box, Packing, Flattened multicolored packing box for Parks Sausage, 16. oz. (cut-down box)

CONTAINER, Box, Packing, Flattened multicolored packing box for Parks Sausage, 16 oz.

CONTAINER, Box, Packing, Flattened multicolored packing box for Parks Sausage, 8 oz.

CONTAINER, Box, Packing, Flattened multicolored packing box for Parks Sausage, 8 oz. with plastic window

DOCUMENTARY ARTIFACT, label, self-sticking paper label w/ backing for Parks Hot Rope Sausage 16 oz.

ADVERTISING MEDIUM, Poster, Small paper advertising stick-up for Parks Pork n' Bacon patties paper

CONTAINER, Pouch, clear, flattened and multicolored plastic pouch for packing Parks Brown n' Serve Scrapple

ADVERTISING MEDIUM, Poster, Stick-up cardboard advertisement for Parks Beef Sausage 2/place for price in upper right corner

CONTAINER, Pouch, clear w/ multicolored label, plastic pouch for packing Parks Very Hot n' Sagey Sausage

CONTAINER, Pouch, Flattened, multicolored pouch for packing Parks Pure Pork Sausage Plastic 24 × 44 cm

CONTAINER, Pouch, Flattened, multicolored pouch for packing Parks Pure Pork Sausage Plastic 24 × 21 cm

CONTAINER, Pouch, Flattened, multicolored plastic pouch for packing Parks Pure Beef Breakfast n' Brunch Sausage

CONTAINER, Pouch, Flattened, multicolored plastic pouch for packing Parks Very Hot n' Sagey Sausage Plastic 24 × 45 cm

CONTAINER, Pouch, Flattened, multicolored plastic pouch for packing Parks Very Hot n' Sagey Pork Sausage Plastic 24 × 21.5 cm

CONTAINER, Pouch, Flattened, multicolored plastic pouch for packing Parks Very Hot n' Sagey Pork Sausage (Parks) Happy Holidays recipe on top center section Plastic 24 × 22 cm

CEREMONIAL ARTIFACT, Tray, Ceremonial "Warner-Lambert Presented Henry G. Parks Jr. For His Dedicated Contributions and Services as a Member of the Board of Directors 1977-1987" Mark Schroth—Handmade sterling 34-14 sterling over metal

CEREMONIAL ARTIFACT, Tray, Ceremonial "Baltimore Junior Association of Commerce/Henry G. Parks/Man of Industry Award/1969/Port and Industrial Development Committee" Mark; EIP YC673 Metal

CEREMONIAL ARTIFACT, Plaque, "Equal Opportunity Award to Henry G. Parks, Junior for Outstanding Contributions Toward The Urban League Goal of Equal Opportunity / Presented March 15, 1964 by Baltimore Urban League" Metal and Wood

CEREMONIAL ARTIFACT, Novelty, "To Henry G. Parks Jr. for Distinguished Service as a Trustee 1963-1969/National Urban League, Inc." Plastic and Metal

ADVERTISING MEDIUM, Novelty, Baltimore Resco Recovery Project/ Wheelabrator-Frye Inc. Plastic

ADVERTISING MEDIUM, Ad, Magazine, "Born to Make Sausage and Scrapple" appeared in *Life* magazine with 2 cents off coupon, attached cardboard stand on back

ADVERTISING MEDIUM, Ad, Magazine "There's a Parks Called . . ." appeared in *Life* magazine, attached cardboard stand on back

CEREMONIAL ARTIFACT, Trowel, "Groundbreaking Ceremony Southwest Recovery Facility," May 2, 1983, Metal and wood

APPENDIX II

Gifts Donated to the Maryland Historical Society Museum and Library of Maryland History by Maurice W. Dorsey, January 15, 1991.

Description of Materials
Prints and Photographs Division
Photographs:

> 1.-16. Gelatin silver prints, roughly 28.0 × 35.3 cm [Interiors of Parks Sausage Plant including manufacturing sausage] [ca. 1965].
> 17.-18 Gelatin silver prints, roughly 20.5 × 45.0 cm [Henry G. Parks at awards banquet], Ruben Hall, photograph [ca.1960] duplicate prints]. Condition: tightly rolled.
> 19. Crayon portrait, roughly 49.5 × 34.5 cm [Henry Parks, Sr.] [ca.1910].

Printed Ephemera

> 1. Certificate of Distinguished Citizenship, the state of Maryland to Henry G. Parks, Award May 25, 1967.
>
> 2. Certificate, The Jefferson Miller Award, Presented to Henry G. Parks Jr. by the Greater Baltimore Committee, April 21, 1983.

APPENDIX III

Gifts Donated to the Maryland Historical Society by Maurice W. Dorsey, August 2, 1991

PLAQUE, 1984, made by A & A Trophy House, MD, metal and wood; engraved award from Delta Lambda Chapter of Alpha Phi Alpha Fraternity Inc. to Brother (Dr.) Henry G. Parks Jr.; Parks was the owner of Parks Sausage, Baltimore

PLAQUE, 1968, unknown maker, metal and wood; engraved award from National Urban League to H. G. Parks Inc.; Parks was the owner of Parks Sausage, Baltimore

PLAQUE, 1977, unknown maker, laminated particle board; award from the United Way of Central Maryland to H. G. Parks Inc.; Parks was the owner of Parks Sausage, Baltimore

PLAQUE, 1973, Kirby-Cogeshall-Steinau Co., Inc. Wisconsin, metal and wood; engraved award from Baltimore Frontier's Club to the Parks Sausage Company; Parks was the owner of Parks Sausage, Baltimore

PLAQUE, 1974, maker unknown, laminated particle board; award from Black Enterprise to H. G. Parks Inc.; Parks was the owner of Parks Sausage, Baltimore

PLAQUE, 1973, maker unknown, laminate particle board; award from Black Enterprise to H. G. Parks Inc.; Parks was the owner of Parks Sausage, Baltimore

PLAQUE, 1967, maker unknown, laminated particle board; advertisement and coupons in McCall's; belonged to Henry G. Parks; Parks was the owner of Parks Sausage, Baltimore

PLAQUE, 1968, made by the Lawrence A. Beck Company, MD, metal and wood; engraved award from the Council for Equal Business Opportunity to Henry G. Parks Jr.; Parks was the owner of Parks Sausage, Baltimore

PLAQUE, 1977, made by Ben Silver Inc., New York, metal and wood; engraved newspaper article from the *New York Times*; reads: "For Henry Parks . . . More Than Sausages"; Parks was the owner of Parks Sausage, Baltimore

PLAQUE, 1972, unknown maker, metal and wood; engraved award from National Urban League Development Foundation to Henry G. Parks Jr.; Parks was the owner of Parks Sausage, Baltimore

PLAQUE, 1972, made by Champion Trophies, Washington, DC, metal and wood; engraved award from United Negro College Fund to Henry G. Parks Jr.; Parks was the owner of Parks Sausage, Baltimore

PLAQUE, 1959, made by L. G. Balfour Co., MA, metal and wood; engraved award from Baltimore Alumni Chapter of Beta Sigma Tau Fraternity to Mr. Henry G. Parks Jr.; Parks was the owner of Parks Sausage, Baltimore

PLAQUE, 1956, unknown maker, metal and wood; engraved Afro-American award to Henry G. Parks; Parks was the owner of Parks Sausage, Baltimore

PLAQUE, 1955, made by Pyraglass, laminated wood; certificate from national Association for the Advancement of Colored People to Henry G. Parks; Parks was the owner of Parks Sausage, Baltimore

PLAQUE, 1964, made by Lawrence A. Beck, MD, metal and wood; engraved award from YMCA of Baltimore to Henry G. Parks Jr.; Parks was the owner of Parks Sausage, Baltimore

PLAQUE, 1963, unknown maker, metal and wood; engraved award from The Small Business Men's League of Baltimore Inc. to Henry G. Parks Jr.; Parks was the owner of Parks Sausage, Baltimore

APPENDIX IV

Original or Photographs from the Private Collection of Maurice W. Dorsey

PLAQUE, 1971, made by Keith Plaques Inc., GA laminated wood; certificate from the Marketing Division of Coca-Cola USA to H. G. Parks Jr.; Parks was owner of the Parks Sausage Company

PLAQUE, 1969, unknown maker, laminated wood; certificate from the Allen and Company Inc. to H. G. Parks Inc.; Parks was owner of the Parks Sausage Company

PLAQUE, 1968, made by Sports Award Company, Illinois, metal and wood; engraved award from Alpha Phi Alpha Fraternity Inc. to Henry G. Parks Jr.; Parks was owner of the Parks Sausage Company

PLAQUE, 1968-1971, unknown maker, metal and wood; engraved award from Metropolitan Transit Authority to Henry G. Parks Jr.; Parks was owner of the Parks Sausage Company

PLAQUE, 1968, made by D & S Nameplate manufacturers, Connecticut, metal and wood; engraved award from the Greater New Haven Business and Professional Men's Association Inc. to Henry G. Parks; Parks was owner of the Parks Sausage Company

PLAQUE, 1966, made by Cooper's Sport Center, PA, metal and wood; engraved ward from the Philadelphia Citizen's Selection Committee to Henry G. Parks Jr.; Parks was owner of the Parks Sausage Company

PLAQUE, 1975, made by Modern Stamp Manufacturing Company, MD, metal and wood; engraved award from Woman Power Inc. to Henry G. Parks; Parks was owner of the Parks Sausage Company

PLAQUE, 1968, unknown maker, laminated wood; advertisement from *Reader's Digest* to H. G. Parks Inc.; Parks was owner of the Parks Sausage Company

PLAQUE, 1971-1974, unknown maker, metal and wood; award from the board of directors of Magnavox Company to Henry G. Park; Parks was owner of the Parks Sausage Company

PLAQUE, 1967, unknown maker, laminated wood; advertisement and coupon from H. G. Parks Inc.

OVAL BOX WITH LID, 1985, made by Solid Brass Specialties, brass; engraved box from Allied Signal; belonged to Henry G. Parks Jr.; Parks was the owner of the Parks Sausage Company

PLAQUE, 1977, unknown maker, plastic from Lehman Brothers Incorporated, announcement of Norin Corporation's financial acquisition of H. G. Parks Inc. Shares of Common Stock; Parks was owner of the Parks Sausage Company

PLAQUE, 1976, unknown maker, plastic; certificate from Service Corps of Retired Executives to Henry G. Parks Jr.; Parks was owner of the Parks Sausage Company

PLAQUE, 1972, unknown maker, clear plastic cube from First Pennsylvania Corporation; belonged to Henry G. Parks; Parks was owner of the Parks Sausage Company

PLAQUE, 1979, unknown maker, medal mounted in plastic; award from Ohio State University's College of Administrative Science to Henry G. Parks; Parks was owner of the Parks Sausage Company

PLAQUE, 1969, unknown maker, 7 coins mounted in plastic; award for valued participation in "Forecast: The 70's"; belonged to Henry G. Parks; Parks was owner of the Parks Sausage Company

PLAQUE, original, the mayor of the City of Baltimore to Henry Parks, as Chairman of the Board of Fire Commissioners, July 12, 1984

PLAQUE, copy, the J. Jefferson Miller Award for Civic Accomplishment, April 1983, by the Greater Baltimore Committee

PLAQUE, original, board of directors, First Pennsylvania Corporation, April 26, 1983, to Henry G. Parks Jr., appreciation to its senior director

PLAQUE, original, the president of the United States to Henry G. Parks Jr., for service on the Executive Committee of the Presidents' Private Sector Survey on Cost Control in the Federal Government, Ronald Reagan, the White House, Washington, DC, September 30, 1983

PLAQUE, original, the comptroller of the City of Baltimore to Honorable Henry Parks Committee on Risk and Insurance Management, December 12, 1983, Hyman Aaron Pressman, comptroller

PLAQUE, original, Alpha Phi Alpha Fraternity Inc. to Henry G. Parks Jr., twenty-five-year membership certificate, March 1, 1982, Ozell Sutton, general president

PLAQUE, original, the Arena Players Inc., board of directors to Henry G. Parks Jr., general campaign chair of the "Possible Dream" 1981 fund-raiser committee, June 12, 1981, Camilla M. Sherrard, chairman of the board of directors

PLAQUE, original, the mayor of the City of Baltimore to Henry G. Parks Jr., as president of the Board of Fire Commissioners, March 11, 1981

PLAQUE, Anne Arundel County, Maryland, in recognition of dedicated service in the cause of human rights, Citizens Award, to Henry G. Parks Jr., Robert A. Pascal, county executive, 1979

PLAQUE, original, proclamation by William Donald Schaefer designating May 18, 1977, as "Henry G. Parks Jr. Day" in Baltimore

PLAQUE, original, the Personnel Association of Greater Baltimore Inc., Scroll of Appreciation for 1977, to Henry G. Parks Jr., May 18, 1977

PLAQUE, original, National Defense University, Industrial College of the Armed Forces presented to Henry G. Parks Jr., class of 1977, major general, United States commandant

PLAQUE, original, Norin Food Products Inc., a wholly owned subsidiary of Norin Corporation, has acquired more than 95 percent of the outstanding common stock of H. G. Parks Inc., May 20, 1977

PLAQUE, original, Henry G. Parks Jr. has been enrolled among the *Shomrei* Israel, November 14, 1976, State of Israel, by Simcha Dinitz, ambassador of the State of Israel to the United States

PLAQUE, original, the Ohio State University Citation for Achievement to Henry G. Parks Jr., November 12, 1973

PLAQUE, original, the Fort McHenry Guard, a proclamation, by the president of the United States, November 3, 1973

PLAQUE, National Alliance of Businessmen to Henry G. Parks Jr., March 1971 and December 4, 1972

PLAQUE, original, the board of directors of the Maryland Crime Investigating Commission to Parks Sausage Co. for combating crime and delinquency

PLAQUE, original, the state of Maryland, to Henry G. Parks Jr. by Marvin Mandel, governor, as member of the Metropolitan Transit Authority, June 30, 1969

PLAQUE, original, state of Maryland Certificate of Election to Henry G. Parks Jr., clerk of the superior court of Baltimore, November 7, 1967

PLAQUE, original, the mayor of the City of Baltimore to Henry G. Parks, as member of the City Council Fourth District, December 7, 1967

PLAQUE, original, Chamber of Commerce of the United States of America to H. G. Parks Inc., as member of the United States Chamber of Commerce, June 30, 1965

PLAQUE, original, the state of Maryland to Henry G. Parks, from the Maryland Commission for the New York World's Fair, 1964-1965, August, 26, 1963

PLAQUE, original, the state of Maryland, Executive Department, citation to Henry G. Parks Jr., Safety Crusader, Safety First Club of Maryland

PLAQUE, original, Alpha Phi Alpha Fraternity Inc., life member, to Henry G. Parks Jr., Chicago, Illinois December 30, 1952

PLAQUE, original, Alpha Phi Alpha Fraternity, membership Kappa Chapter, Columbus, Ohio, April 25, 1936

PLAQUE, original, Certificate of Membership to Henry Parks, member of the National Athletic Scholarship Society of Secondary Schools, no date

Copy of Birth Certificate from the state of Georgia, 1982

Photograph collection of Henry at the Defense Personnel Support Center, 1975

Photograph collection of Henry at Temple University, receiving honorary doctorate, 1975

Photograph collection at Defense Supply Agency, Philadelphia, 1975

Photograph collection of Henry on *Time* Magazine Southeast Asia News Tour

Photograph collection from Allied Signal Corporation, 1978

Photograph of "More Parks' Sausages, Mom, Please!" on banner flying over Fenway Park, Boston, Boston versus New York Yankees, 1978

Photographs of Baltimore Metropolitan Alliance of Businessmen, 1972

Photograph collection of family

Photograph collection of City Council years, 1960s

Photograph collection color and black-and-white Foster and Kleiser billboards lining New York City Streets, Bronx, Manhattan, Brooklyn, and Queens, 1960s and 1970s

Photograph collection of United States Air Force in Vietnam, Cam Ranh Bay Air Base, March 1969

Photograph collection of the Philadelphia Citizens Selection Committee, October 1966

Photographs in this Book

Photograph, Henry in childhood, the Corbitt Studio, 127 South Main Street Dayton, Ohio

Photograph, Henry, Roosevelt High School Class of 1934

Photograph, Henry, 1938

Photograph, Jeanne Parks, Henry's sister

Photograph, Vera Parks Wilson, Henry's sister

Photograph, Henry and Virginia Byrd wedding

Photograph, Grace, Virginia, and Cheryl

Photograph, Henry at office on Hamburg Street

Photograph, Henry campaigning for Baltimore City Council, Fourth District

Photograph, Fannie Jones, Henry, and Ethel Rich, 1963

Photograph, Henry on Council bench, 1963

Photograph, Councilmen Henry, Thomas J. D'Alesandro III, William Donald Schaefer

Photograph, Foster and Kleiser billboard at Tremont and Third, 1968

BIBLIOGRAPHY

____, An Adventure in Business Cooperation, A business owned and controlled by Negros, The Parks Sausage Company, Pittsburgh, Pennsylvania, *The Pittsburgh Courier*, February 16, 1952

____, Sausage Success, Negro Firm in Baltimore Proves American System in World's Best, Chicago, Illinois, *Sepia* magazine, July 1955

____, Who Will Be Crowned Chitterling King or Queen at D. C. first Chitterling Eating Contest & Feast, Washington, DC, *The Washington Spotlight*, January 14, 1955

____, Opportunity's Door is Open to Enterprise, Chicago, Illinois, *The National Provisioner*, May 5, 1956

____, Parks Famous Flavor Comes To Chicago, *Chicago Sunday Tribune*, January 26, 1958

____, Parks Sausages Advertise on WITH Radio, Baltimore, Maryland, *Food World*, February, 1958

____, Regular or Hot and Sagey!, *The Daily Defender*, Chicago, Illinois, February 20, 1958

____, Sausage Talk, Chicago, Illinois, *Jet* magazine, March 6, 1958

____, Ladies Day Lunch, the Parks Sausage Hour, Detroit, Michigan, *Michigan Chronicle*, April 5, 1958

____, Courier Home Services Show, Philadelphia, Pennsylvania, *Philadelphia Tribune*, April 29, 1958

____, Cotillian to Honor Roy Wilkins, Edward Brooks, Henry Parks, New York, New York, *New York Courier*, December 14, 1963

____, Ten Top Radio Commercials Named in Pulse Study for Blair Radio, New York, New York, *Sponsor*, February 25, 1963

____, Blair Announces 'top10' radio spot, New York, New York, *Broadcasting*, February 25, 1963

____, Advertising Age, BBDO Radio Ads for Dodge, Pepsi Cited in Top 10, Chicago, Illinois, February 25, 1963

____, Senate, Washington, DC, *Congressional Record*, December 6, 1963

____, Negro in Business Rather than a Negro businessman, Jersey City, New Jersey, *The Jersey Journal and Jersey Observer*, November 18, 1963

_____, Packaging and Spice Add Variety to Pork Sausage Product, Chicago, Illinois, the *National Provisioner*, November 21, 1964

_____, Publisher of Supplement to Be Honored, Philadelphia, Pennsylvania, the *Evening Bulletin*, September 29, 1966

_____, A Negro Integrates His market, New York, New York, *Business Week*, May 18, 1968

_____, Henry G. Parks Jr. Get Top Award at the Philadelphia Citizen Selection Committee Fifth Annual Award, Philadelphia, Pennsylvania, *the Philadelphia Tribune*, October 15, 1966

_____, Parks Sausage in $1 Million Plant; Enters 'Second Phase', Baltimore, Maryland, the Baltimore *Afro-American*, March 11, 1967

_____, Henry A Knott, Inc. Creative Building, Baltimore, Maryland, *Baltimore* magazine, April 1967

_____, "More Parks Sausages, Mom!" Baltimore, Maryland, *Baltimore Economic Development Digest*, May, 1967

_____, Processor Just Grows and Grows, Chicago, Illinois, the *Provisioner*, May 6, 1967

_____, Baltimore Businessman Henry G. Parks Jr., a Negro Integrates His Market, *Business Week*, May 18, 1968

_____, The Nation's 100 Top Black Businesses, New York, New York, *Black Enterprise*, June, 1973

_____, Black Directors, The 72 Black Men and Women Who Sit On The Boards of Major US Corporations, New York, New York, *Black Enterprise*, September 1973

_____, Top 100, New York, New York, *Black Enterprise*, June 1974

_____, Top 100, New York, New York, *Black Enterprise*, June 1975

_____, Detroit Firm and Parks Hold Talks, Baltimore, Maryland, the *Baltimore Sun*, November 7, 1975

_____, H.G. Parks Weighs Merger against Loss of Its Black Identity, Meat Concern Ponders Joining Frederick & Herrud to Assure Source of Supply, New York, New York, the *Wall Street Journal*, November 7, 1975

_____, Fifty Leading Black Businesses in Maryland, Baltimore, Maryland, the *Baltimore Sun*, November 20, 1985

_____, Parks, Smale Feted at Annual UNCF Gala Held in New York City, New, New York, *Jet* magazine, April 6, 1987

_____, Parks Sausage Co. Founder Henry G. Parks, 72, Dies, Chicago, Illinois, *Jet* magazine, May 15, 1989

Bill Bridge, Negro Must Enter Business, Industry, League Told, Mamaroneck, New York, *Daily Times*, December 5, 1967

Art Carter, Black Olympians, They Were the Best Paving the Way for the Rest, Baltimore, Maryland, the *Baltimore Afro-American*, February 14, 1987

Ralph P. Davidson, Time News Tour Group, a Letter from the Publisher, Chicago, Illinois, *Time*, February 10, 1975

John Dorsey, Henry Parks: The Man behind the Sausage, Baltimore, Maryland, the *Baltimore Sun* magazine, July 27, 1975

Martin Evans, Maryland's Best Crowd Funeral of Henry Parks, Baltimore, Maryland, Friends crowd businessman's funeral as daughter offers a touching eulogy, the *Baltimore Sun*, April 28, 1989

Norman H. Fischer, Retail Pork Prices, Up 40% in Year, Are Expected to Rise Even Further, New York, New York, the *Wall Street Journal*, September 19, 1975

Michael A. Fletcher, Rites Thursday for Henry G. Parks, Jr., Baltimore, Maryland, the *Baltimore Sun*, April 25, 1989

Lawrence Freeny, For Henry Parks . . . More Than Sausages, New York, New York, the *New York Times*, April 10, 1977

James Grant, Parks Sausage Ad Rankled-But Sold, Baltimore, Maryland, the *Baltimore Sun*, January 19, 1975

James Grant, Parks Earnings Rebound Sharply, Baltimore, Maryland, the *Baltimore Sun*, February 5, 1975

Nancy Greenberg, Parks: Sausage and the Man, Philadelphia, Pennsylvania, the *Evening Bulletin*, May 30, 1975

David L Himelfarb, Call It Politics, Baltimore, Maryland, *Labor Herald*, March 10, 1967

William Hyder, Father-And-Son Commercial, Baltimore, Maryland, *the Baltimore Sun*, July 25, 1965

Bradford Jacobs, "Got to Get One" Baltimore, Maryland, *the Baltimore Sun*, January 1966

Bob Lockett, the Remarkable Henry Parks, This is a wonderful story of a man who is blazing a trail for black businessmen of tomorrow, Baltimore, Maryland, the *Baltimore Sun*, 1968

Douglas W. Clay, Mr. Parks' $10 Million Recipe, Man on the Move Henry G. Parks, Jr., Baltimore, Maryland, *Signature*, July 1972

Welford L. McLellan, Black Capitalism: Color It Green, Baltimore, Maryland, *Baltimore, magazine*, May 1970

Carl Murphy, Letter of Congratulations, Baltimore, Maryland, *Afro-American Newspapers*, February 4, 1952

Henry G. Parks, Jr., Successful Business Operations, Washington, DC, Howard University, October 1966

Jack Hodge, Parks Sausages Grow Into Industrial Park, Baltimore Maryland, the *News American*, March 12, 1967

Jeanne Saddler, How to Become a Millionaire: Henry G. Parks Gives His Rules For Success, Meat Products firm he founded now has record annual sales, Chicago, Illinois, *Ebony*, March 1977

Alisa Samuels and Charles H. Brown, 800 Attend Rites for H. G. Parks, 72, Baltimore, Maryland, the *Baltimore Afro-American*, April 29, 1989

David Schwartz, Introduction to Management: Principles, Practices, and Processes, New York, New York, *Harcourt Brace Jovanovich, Inc.*, 1980

David Segal, Parks Sausages Co. Ask Maryland for Help, Baltimore Firm Says $8 Million Needed to Stay I Operation, Washington, DC, the *Washington Post*, July 15, 1995

David Segal, Former Football Star to Buy Parks Sausage Co., Washington, DC, the *Washington Post*, June 22, 1996

Ralph Simpson, Henry Parks is Black and Proud, Baltimore, Maryland, the *Baltimore Sun*, October 3, 1971

Anson Smith, Risking Millions a Venture in American Capitalism, Boston, Massachusetts, *Boston Globe*, October 8, 1978

Jane A. Smith and Dennis O'Brian, Henry Parks, Civil Rights and Business Leader, Dies, Baltimore, Maryland, the *Baltimore Sun*, April 25, 1989

Joe Smith, the Sales Scene, Baltimore, Maryland, *Antenna*, March 1964

Wilson Sullivan, Its Tuesday on Sundays, Chicago, Illinois, *SR*, November 13, 1965

Roger Twigg, Fire Board Alters Policy on Promotion, Aim is to Give Blacks More High-level jobs, Baltimore, Maryland, the *Baltimore Sun*, November 16, 1983

Mildred Weiler Tyson, Idea plus Effort pays Off for Black, Boston, Massachusetts, the *Christian Science Monitor*, 1969

LIST OF ILLUSTRATIONS

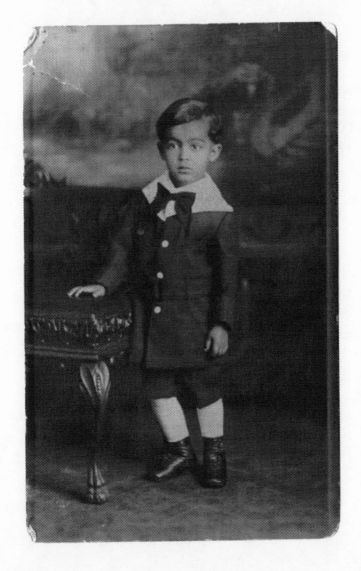

Henry in childhood

Henry, Roosevelt High School Class of 1934

Henry, 1938

Jeanne Parks, Henry's sister

Vera Parks Wilson

Henry and Virginia Byrd wedding

Grace, Virginia, and Cheryl

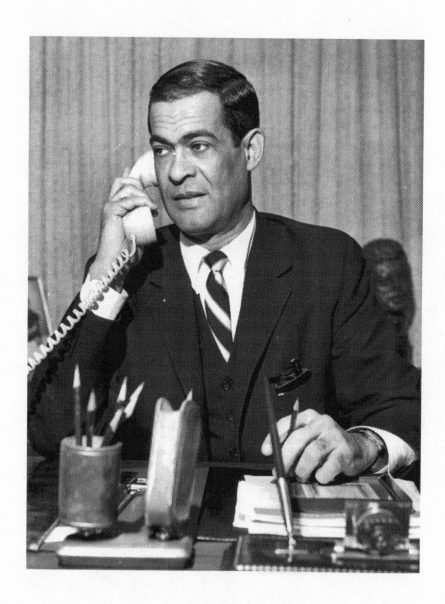

Henry at office on Hamburg Street

Henry campaigning for Baltimore City Council, Fourth District

Fannie Jones, Henry, and Ethel Rich

Henry on Council bench

Councilmen Henry, Thomas J. D'Alesandro III, William Donald Schaefer

Foster and Kleiser billboard at Tremont and Third, 1968 New York